Inner *In* *Being* *Balance*

7 Principles for Manifesting Success in Life, Business and Beyond

MONICA W. GRAVES

BALBOA.PRESS

A DIVISION OF HAY HOUSE

Balboa Press books may be ordered through booksellers or by contacting:

Balboa Press
A Division of Hay House
1663 Liberty Drive
Bloomington, IN 47403
www.balboapress.com
844-682-1282

Cover Image Credit: Michael B. Graves

Print information available on the last page.

ISBN: 978-1-9822-5954-9 (sc)
ISBN: 978-1-9822-5957-0 (e)

Balboa Press rev. date: 12/17/2020

Monica has a personality that is beautiful and vibrant, and I can connect with her easily. - Jill Mant

"Monica is such a fun and vibrant soul. She is truly a living example of her work and the work she has done in her own life. Her workshops are full of creative and fun ways to create the life of your dreams. I have used her tools and she has help shift my life into what it is today. I am forever grateful for Monica and the gifts she has to offer." -Miss Dannie Huggs
Intuitive Guide and Healer

Cheers to Monica Wilson Graves! I've been fortunate and blessed to have taken many of her classes and workshops, shared incredible life changing experiences, and have enjoyed a long friendship with Monica. She simply walks her talk. I've loved watching her create and continue to manifest a balanced and happy life of her dreams! Her Ninja classes have assisted hundreds of realtors and helped me personally with training techniques to boost my sales quotas, in shifting my mindset, and living a life of gratitude. Her support of my music and life choices has been unfailing. Monica's commitment to truth teachings, her love for knowledge, the way she listens and easy way she communicates, makes her a wonderful teacher and workshop facilitator! You're in for a treat! ~ Terri Vigneulle James

Happiness is not a matter of intensity, but of balance, order, rhythm, and harmony. Thomas Merton

Dedication

My soulmate, Michael, who helped me discover balancing my Inner Being, by just being himself.

Contents

Foreword

by Larry Kendall, Author of Ninja Selling

What does it mean to live with inner balance? Monica Graves shows you the way. Her seven simple principles provide you with a roadmap to aligning your mind, body, and spirit. Her book is filled with exercises designed to help you discover who you really are so you can achieve the results you want in your life.

Monica's personal journey of exploration and learning is fascinating. She has lived every principle she teaches, has faced many challenges, and has achieved incredible success. She is her own science project. And now, fortunately, she is sharing her experiences and knowledge in this book, in her quest to help you live a better, more balanced life.

I know Monica as an amazing teacher, coach, writer, computer scientist, fashion designer, entrepreneur, investor, salesperson, poet, athlete, and mom. She has a big picture perspective on life and what it takes to be successful. In addition to the science, philosophy, and self-discovery that you will learn from her, Monica's personal life story is an inspiration and reason alone to read this book.

As Monica says, "In any given moment we have two options: to step forward into growth or to step backward into safety." Are you committed to be the best possible version of yourself? Then step forward into the *Inner Being in Balance.*

Preface

What would your life look like if you were truly happy? Imagine what it feels like to be happy with your life's work. Instead of living with worry, fear, and guilt, your life is full of complete joy and a sense of balance. That balance is the path to having happiness in every living moment. The reward for having a life balance is often called *Nirvana*. If you've ever dreamed of having better inner balance or following your passion and creating the life you were meant to live, now you can make that dream come true.

Why I Wrote This Book

I was allowing my worthiness to be determined by someone else, not me. My health was suffering, and the constellation of all my experiences was lining up to become the map of my life. I needed to heal and love *me* before I could heal and love others. I needed to change my thinking, to change the course of where my life was headed. I needed balance in my life. My past experiences gave me the stepping-stones I needed to create the work and life I love. I feel these steps can help and heal others.

I wrote this book because I have had many amazing experiences in my life, good and bad. I have noticed that when I share my stories, many people can relate to them and can be made more aware and also healed. I am writing this book to share my stories in the hope that I can reach even more people who may learn and have a healing work–life experience.

You see, we all have talents, and all of us are gifted with our own originality and creativity. But some people may not be using their special talents in the everyday field of making money. Some may even hate their jobs, but they continue to get up and go to a work activity that is actually making them sick. And if you are like me, you would rather be healthy than be given any amount of a paycheck that the job provides.

This book will help you to see that you can have it all: a happy job, a happy life, and your inner being in balance.

Finding Balance

Inner Being in Balance uses an acronym to help you remember the recommended daily habits and put them to practice.

BALANCE

Believing
Allowing
Learning
Affirming
Nurturing
Celebrating
Expanding

I have worked with these seven principles for the past twenty-seven years. I have noticed amazing changes in my life, and the work that is my passion was created. I discovered how to have inner balance as a working mother and wife. I found the courage to change. After years of guilt, worry, and stress, I learned to follow my passion, try new ways of thinking, express myself creatively, and share my own voice to help others to learn what I have learned.

Life is all about Metaphysical Principles.

The Power of Spirit is inside of us. It's called our Inner Being. It is not outside of us.

When we feel separate from others, we are not living our deepest truth. We are actually disempowering ourselves. You have heard the saying; build your house on sand or build your house on rock. You are building your house on sand, if you are not surrounding yourself with a strong belief from the inside. You are building your house on rock, if you know the ultimate truth that the Power of Spirit is inside you, not on the outside.

Also, the Ultimate Truth is; there is no time or space. This is a part of the human Illusion. There is no place where you start and where I finish. We All connected to the same Reality. Ernest Holmes says, "You can only achieve what you can conceive." On the Spiritual Realm, there is no give and take, there is just giving and receiving. You must be open to receiving.

When you wake up, ask these questions to your Inner Being;

"Where would you have me go today?"

"What would you have me do?"

"Who would you have me meet?"

"What would you have me say?"

"Use me to the highest and best that I can be!"

It is not up to you, what you need to learn, because we learn through either pain or joy. There is no order of difficulty in "Miracles". Spiritual Power lies in all circumstances where there is an unlimited amount of love. We can say this, "I am not created in the effect of Lovelessness, I am created in the full potential of unlimited love."

Enlightenment is a journey of responding positively to error. Miracles don't happen in the past, they happen in the present. Anytime, the mind is not used in the present, the programming of your future will happen no matter what, so live in the now and miracles will happen. Our only experience on earth that is real, is to "give love and receive love". Don't get attached to outcomes, just be present and positive with faith and a belief that, "All is Well."

In living authentically with the "Winners Edge" mindset; Creating things from the inside out. People will like you and want to do business with you, because of your positivity and they can feel it. It's not just about your Resume', it's about who you really are.

"Miracles" are how you can be used in life for service. Remember, an idea is stronger when it is shared. Find something in life that you can be of service and share your beliefs. Be aware. Be of value. Be You.

My Notes 9/27/2013 – Centers For Spiritual Living, Lakewood, CO
Marianne Williamson – The Law fo Divine Compensation

Introduction

The camera was inserted down my throat, through my esophagus, and into my stomach. The TV screen hooked to the camera showed me and the doctors corroded, puss-filled ulcers of fear. At that moment, I asked myself out loud, "*That's* what I look like inside?"

The doctor heard me and answered, "Yes. It's pretty nasty!"

Pretty nasty. Those two words stuck with me for years, and I will never forget them because that was exactly how I felt: pretty on the outside and nasty on the inside. I was living an unbalanced life—a life that was a lie. My body had decided the truth needed to be revealed. It needed to be displayed for me on a camera and TV monitor so that I could see my insides on the outside.

I was thirty-five years old, and I had spent eleven years mistreating my body with alcohol, drugs, and stress. It was time for me to wake up and pay attention. It was time for me to become aware. Why was I so out of balance? Why did I do this to myself? Why was I in this situation filled with fear?

These questions led me to seek answers from books, tapes, workshops on healing—anything I could get my hands on that could help me to heal physically, emotionally, and spiritually. I started a Kundalini yoga class filled with chanting and breathing. I learned to slow down and live in the moment, and I quit my high-paying position in the corporate world and moved from the fast-paced energy of New York to a small town called Golden, Colorado.

I have always been a person who wants the best out of life, and I have always had the driven mindset that I can have whatever I want. The problem was that, while I was definitely creating everything I *thought* I wanted, I got very out of balance with my health, my wealth, and my career. I hope that I can help people learn from the mistakes I made. I've learned that there is a much easier way.

When I was only twenty-two, I got married to my soul mate. Three months later, I got a job with a huge fashion designer and moved to New York City. My husband said "Go for it," and he stayed behind in Atlanta to finish his engineering degree. Well, seven years later, I was still working in New York, and he was still left behind in Georgia. We thought we were on top of the world because we were making so much money, but in fact, we had way too much debt and way too much stress.

I became very sick from working so many hours and not eating or drinking right, and before I knew it, I was in the hospital with twenty-two ulcers. I started reading the book *You Can Heal Your Life* by Louise Hay, and it changed my life forever. You see, I needed to look at the emotions behind my dis-ease, and regarding ulcers, *Heal Your Life* has this to say: "Extreme Worry that you are Not Good Enough."

At first, I didn't get this. I thought, *Of course I think I am good enough; that is why I work so many hours and work so hard for this famous designer.* But soon, as I looked closer to the way I was working and the way I was living, I saw that I *was* out of balance. My inner balance was way off with my outer balance. I realized I needed to love *me* first and my job second. Once I realized that I didn't really love the job and that I loved me more, I quit. I left a high-paying prestigious job working in a high-fashion house in New York and moved back to Atlanta to be with my husband and two little boys.

Here's what happened after that. I started my own merchandising company, became an independent contractor for several fashion houses, and also got my real estate license. I realized at that moment that I was the only one in control of what I wanted and that I had to have a balance between my work and my life. I am now a real estate agent, real estate agent coach, and inner balance instructor. Every day, I see that my thinking creates my reality. And my reality is exactly what I want it be, without all the stress, the debt, and the sickness.

I had made the decision to listen to my fearless intuition. As I became less fearful, my life became more balanced and fuller of love. I started *believing* in myself and letting go of false beliefs I had about abundance. I was *allowing* my mind to be open to trust for the first time. I was *learning* every day that positive affirmations were changing my life. I started *affirming* only those things that I really wanted in life, and soon they were manifesting. I tried *nurturing* myself with the best foods and exercising every day. I was *celebrating* me and all that I had manifested. And, most important, I was *expanding* my thoughts and being an expressive and loving individual who had found her purpose. I realized that loving myself and approving of myself was the most important lesson that had to happen to truly heal and balance my inner being.

I have faith that if you do the same, you too can live in balance. I am a licensed Heal Your Life workshop leader and also a certified Ninja Selling instructor. Not only do I lead workshops and teach mindset classes, but I also have a thriving real estate business, where I am an employing broker and manage and train hundreds of real estate agents. My husband and son work with me, and we love our work–life experience.

Over the past twenty-seven years, I have used the power of manifestation to create the life of my dreams. This included becoming more spiritual and using positive thinking to help me experience more of what I truly wanted. I learned the power of my thoughts and how they can take form to create the reality I was envisioning. Our thoughts truly affect how we experience our own reality, and by believing that, you can easily change your thoughts.

Knowing that I could change my life, I realized that what I thought and what I felt every single day would determine how my reality would be. That's why I decided to write this book, and I believe it's the reason you are now reading this book. Somewhere in your subconscious, you desire change. My change was that I needed more inner balance. After being so sick and living with so much stress, I knew my body, mind, and spirit needed a new reality.

I want you to know how I learned to listen to my inner being. I want you to know that your mind has higher abilities and a higher power than you may even realize. According to the law of attraction, written about by many spiritual leaders and life coaches, you attract into your life what you focus your attention on—positive or negative. The content of your thoughts will define and manifest your reality.

This concept of manifesting what you truly desire begins with how you respond to life events and take responsibility for your thoughts. You can learn from every single life event that is happening to you, good or bad. By taking responsibility and knowing that you control your thoughts and can change those thoughts, you allow your true self to emerge, versus the conditional self that has programmed your mind to have certain beliefs.

If your wish or desire, like mine, is to manifest more balance in your life, then you will need to understand and accept the manifestation process first. It starts with imagination. Albert Einstein said, "Imagination is more important than knowledge." Imagination opens the door to your inner being and leads you to more awareness. What you imagine can become true for you. Feel how it feels to have what you want.

When imagining and visualizing, you must believe that it will work for you. You must believe that it is already your reality. We will talk more about believing and your programming in the chapter called "Believing." Instead of saying, "I'll believe it when I see it," say, "I'll see it when I believe it." Believe it is possible, and it will be. Believing you deserve something makes manifesting easier.

Now take a good look at your limiting beliefs and how they affect your life. If you believe something will be hard to achieve, it definitely will be difficult. If you believe that something like balancing your life can be easily achieved, you will be in tune with that belief, and it will be a lot easier to achieve.

In the chapter called "Allowing," we will talk about how you can allow the universe to bring you more of what you desire. But first, you have to eliminate your programmed, conditioned, self-imposed limits. When releasing old habits or old beliefs, you will begin to open your mind to new beliefs and new habits. If you can believe it, you can achieve it.

In the chapter called "Learning," we will discuss how you can apply what you learn every day from life events and use a positive belief mindset to attract more positivity into any area of your life, whether it's health, wealth, your job, your relationships or anything you desire. It is very important to learn how to serve others and find your purpose.

Once you learn how the manifesting process works, pay attention to how you feel. Putting a feeling on something you are focusing on will give it more energy. We are all made up of energy. Energy is vibrational, so changing your thoughts to a higher vibration and using the power of feeling helps the manifesting process.

In the chapter called "Affirming," we will talk about how feeling the affirmation gives it more power. You can use positive feelings around the affirmations to create a vibrational match. This vibrational act will align you with the universe, and the universe will give back to you what you desire in your affirmation. Affirmations always need to be positive so that a positive feeling and a positive vibration will be the outcome.

As you continue to learn and use the power of manifesting, you will start to understand how important it is to nurture your body as well as your mind and spirit. In the chapter called "Nurturing," we will discuss how important it is to take care of your health. A healthy person will attract on a higher frequency than a person who is always sick. The manifesting process is harder for someone who is attracting with a negative vibration. The good thing to know is that the power of manifesting to be well and heal yourself is truly possible. But it starts with loving and nurturing yourself first.

Once you love and forgive yourself, you must be consistent with these thoughts. Focusing on the power of self-love is the highest vibrational energy that a human can have. Nurturing this power of self-love will help to heal any sickness, and the manifestation process will become easier and easier. As you continue to align more with the universe and manifest what you desire, balancing your life becomes more of a celebration of life.

In the chapter called "Celebrating," we discuss together how important it is to celebrate a new goal achieved, because you now have proven that manifestation works. Celebrating is the highest form of being grateful. By being grateful, you will attract more things into your life to be grateful for. Try waking up in the morning and think of three things that you are grateful for. Celebrate those things in your life, and more of the same will be manifested into your life. Try thinking of three new things every day to celebrate and be grateful for.

We all have amazing things that happen to us. We have become complacent and take things for granted. For example, one person may not have public access to a toilet, so if given the opportunity to use one, they would feel blessed and grateful for that toilet. Other people might never think of the toilet as something to be grateful for, because they use it daily. So think of how many things there are in your life that you can celebrate. Make a list in a gratitude journal and become aware of all the good.

The last chapter in this book is called "Expanding." Once your inner being is more in balance and you are matching vibrationally with the universe, you will be in the realm of expanding. Your thoughts, which are created in your brain, have the ability to send out a frequency, because physically, your thoughts send out nerve impulses throughout your body. Your positive thoughts expand out and send a positive vibration that will be more powerful with feeling an emotion. So, in essence, when you have a positive feeling or emotion about something, you are actually expanding your environment, and all the positive vibrations that are connected to it will also be positive.

Your physical body, as well as your spiritual expansion, aligns you more and more with the universe. Remember, the universe and you are one. You and the universe are connected. So, as you expand your positive vibrations, the outcome you receive back into your reality will be more positive as well.

Look at the word *universe*. It is made up of two Latin words: *uni*, meaning "one," and *verses*, meaning "turning into." Literally, it means "one turned into." So, if you think about it, the universe is everything. It is one energy, and we are part of that one energy. Just as we are all the same energy, we also share universal consciousness. We are all connected to this universal consciousness, so by expanding our thoughts on creation and manifestation, we are attracting that same frequency back to us within the universal consciousness.

Expanding is a form of channeling. The more you expand your thinking, the easier it is to channel the things you desire into your life. Just know that you are part of something bigger and more expansive, like the universe, and believe that the universe wants exactly what you want. If you want balance in your life, health, wealth, joy, and happiness, then all you have to do is remember to stay aligned with the universe. Do not say no to the universe; just say yes, because every event in your life is how you are communicating and channeling your thoughts between you and the universe. This is how you find inner being balance.

In my work as a real estate coach and life coach, I am often reminded that what works for some people does not necessarily work for all people, so each person may have a different idea of what balance means to them. I hope that by addressing the word *balance* and also different areas in which the word can help you, that you will find what works best for you.

What does being in balance mean to you? Being in balance to me means aligning with the universe to manifest less chaos, less stress, and more calm. I am grounded but also more motivated.

The seven steps I have outlined in this book will describe what the word *balance* means to me. We will spell out *BALANCE* with each letter of the word broken down to remember the habits more easily: *B* for believing, *A* for allowing, *L* for learning, *A* for affirming, *N* for nurturing, *C* for celebrating, and *E* for expanding.

Having your inner being in balance completely and perfectly may be a goal in life that can never truly be achieved, because we are always evolving. But with the knowledge that we are always growing, always changing, and always choosing, we can use these seven steps to help us manifest our best life and become our best selves by being better with inner balance.

What is your inner being? It is who you really are on the inside. To know your inner being is to know your purpose, values, vision, goals, motivations, and beliefs—not what you have been told by others but what you have discovered for yourself. Knowing and balancing your inner being requires a high level of introspection and self-awareness.

We all know that there are times when life is a balancing act. We may feel that we are just one step from falling and crashing. It can feel chaotic, because we are constantly trying to find our purpose, achieve our goals, and balance the other elements of our lives with relationships and external things. Since we are all energy, and our lives are how we use that energy, sometimes we have to give up something to get something. We feel we must deal with areas in our lives that are taking up too much of our energy so we can maintain an inner balance with the outer balance.

How do we do this without creating more chaos in our lives? The answer is, start with inner balance first. It is very important to understand that other people cannot do this for us. No one else can think for us, breathe for us, or live for us. We are in charge of our own inner balance, and it is up to us to make the changes needed to create the life of our dreams. We just have to decide to do it.

Congratulations on finding and reading this book. The commitment to learn something new and make life changes takes courage. Now, let's dive in and manifest the life of your dreams.

CHAPTER 1

Believing

We are the ones who invest seemingly bad happenings
with the power to seem bad at the time they occurred, to
continue to seem bad afterwards. William Shakespeare

With believing, I want you to ask yourself two questions: "Who am I, and what do I believe?" Have you ever just sat there and contemplated these questions? This book is written to explore these types of questions so that you can change some of the limiting beliefs you may have, consciously or unconsciously, programmed yourself to believe. If you are willing to change some of your thoughts, then you can actually change your life.

If you have positive beliefs, then I encourage you to keep them and just expand on them; we will talk about expanding later in the book. If you find that you have negative beliefs, then I believe this book will help you to release them and just let them go. The steps outlined in this book can help you to align with the universe and manifest the life you truly love. My life is a great example of overcoming negative beliefs.

For years, my belief was that I was never good enough. Sound familiar? At a very early age, I was treated as the wild child who needed discipline. My father used physical, as well as, verbal punishment to try to force me to behave as he thought I should. I would get beaten with a belt or a switch

1

from a tree—and then told not to cry or I would get hit again. Holding back the crying was probably the hardest part for me.

Not only did my father discipline me like this, but his parents, my paternal grandparents, would also use these methods of abuse. I am sure that it was passed down from their parents and so on, for hundreds of years. But guess what? It all ended with me. I decided that I would not use these physical beatings to discipline my own children. I knew it did not work. It did not work to discipline me; all it did, as I was growing up, was make me feel that I was a bad person.

The belief of never being good enough was part of the programming that created negative beliefs about myself. I was always trying to show that I could be good, but my programming beliefs that I could never be good enough would always be there subconsciously to bring me back down. I continued to be an overachiever.

Things started to change when my parents divorced and my father moved out of state. His parents, my paternal grandparents, were also no longer a part of my life. I was around eleven years old at this time. I was very mature for my age, and I decided then that I could be and do whatever I wanted. But over and over, until I was fifty-three years old, my negative beliefs would cause my physical health to diminish, as well as my mental and spiritual health.

This spiraled me down to the lowest part of my life. It was at this point that I was shown, by listening more closely to my inner being, that I needed to forgive my parents, forgive my grandparents, and most importantly, forgive myself. I immersed myself in self-love. I became a certified Heal Your Life teacher with Louise Hay, one of the pioneers of self-development. I am now happy to say that I am healthy, wealthy, and very grateful for everything I have learned. I realized I needed to share my story with the hope that it would help others.

Here is what I have learned about life and what I believe. Life is what you make it! Your thoughts create your life. Thoughts are just things, and thoughts can be changed. Each of us creates our life experience by our thoughts. The thoughts we think and the words we speak are beliefs or ideas we have learned. "Our thoughts are what we accept as the truth," says Louise Hay, "and what we think about ourselves and the world becomes true for us."

What each of us chooses to believe can expand our world or shrink our world. Two people living in the same world, and even born from the same parents, with the same set of life circumstances, can experience life so differently. Our belief system makes it so.

Ask yourself, again, "What do I believe?" Are there things in your life you want to change and improve? Do you want more balance? Are you willing to change? Well, if you are willing to change some of your primary belief structures, then yes, you can change your life, and you can align yourself with the universe to help you create a life you truly love.

Remember, your beliefs about yourself and the life you desire are just thoughts, and thoughts can be changed. You can always choose again. We have unlimited choices about what we think, and our subconscious mind accepts them, whatever we choose to believe. The universe will never judge you or criticize you for your beliefs. It just accepts you for what you believe and will attract to you more of that belief.

So if you choose to believe you are a victim and there is no hope for you, the universe will support you in this belief. But if you can change those thoughts and beliefs to knowing you have choices, you are responsible for your life experiences, and you believe you deserve the best life, then the universe will support you in this belief as well. So aligning with the universe is a good choice and a good positive belief system.

This is the first step in having better balance in your life and for manifesting the life of your wildest dreams. Say this out loud before we move on: "I believe I have the power to change." This is an important affirmation, and we will talk more about affirmations in another chapter.

The first step in manifesting balance and gaining true alignment with your goals or your divine purpose is to let go of fear. Believing in yourself and being in the moment, when you're looking at your goals, is so important. Too many times we allow our past programming and past conditions to bring fear into our present moment. Fear of failing—of investing time, money, and energy and not succeeding—can cloud our vision of what we truly desire.

Fear can keep you frozen. When you are centered and aligning yourself in the present moment, fear cannot exist in that moment. Letting go of fear is like letting go of the past. It is a feeling of peace, of being grounded with sanity, and of assurance. When you are centered and balanced, you can open your heart fearlessly to what life is bringing you. It pushes you closer to your goals and lets you know there is nothing that can knock you off balance.

You don't need to look for answers outside of yourself. There is no need for worry or anxiety. When you are in true alignment, centered and balanced, you will become more aware of the inspiration that can guide you to your true purpose and accomplish goals in wondrous new ways. Just centering yourself in love and the present moment will let fear disappear. I believe that every one of us has the goal of being happy. But happiness is an inside job. We must be happy and love ourselves first before we can attract more happiness.

What are your dreams? What are your goals? How do you manifest them into being? Why have you not received what you truly desire in your life? These are all questions that you may be asking yourself. By reading this book, you are on your way to learning how to create inner balance and align with the universe to attract the life you have always dreamed of.

Cocreating on a daily basis with the seven habits outlined in this book will help you manifest your wildest dreams. For the past twenty-seven years, I have been a seeker of truth, of the answer to the question "What is my purpose?" or "What is my calling?"—or, biggest of all, "Why am I here?" When I was younger, these questions and my curiosity were stifled by the religion that was part of my upbringing. I was told not to ask questions and that God would take care of everything. In a sense, this is true, but the God of my religion was a judging God, an angry God who would punish you for wrongdoing. We needed to remember that if we didn't follow the rules outlined in this religion, we would go to this terrible place called hell.

This religion was based on fear of God, not so much on a loving God. That is why I had so many questions. If something terrible happened to me or to anyone, the answer was always, "It must be in God's plan." I was being told that I really didn't have free will and that my future was already ordained by the will of a judging God. Judgment day was my future, and I needed to be afraid, so that I would do "God's will."

As I write this, that same old feeling of fear is still in my subconscious or the part of my brain that remembers all the fear. I am sure the majority of you who are reading this book have the same memory of living with fear, because fear was taught as the way to believe in most religions. We are born into this world full of love, and fear is taught to us as we grow. So, it's really a huge part of our programming by the time we are adults. Our ego, or our self-talk, is so based on fear that love is pushed aside. As Marianne Williamson in her book, *A Return to Love* expressed so truthfully, "Fear is the absence of Love."

> *Our happiness depends on the habit of mind*
> *we cultivate. Norman Vincent Peale*

Believing everything that has ever happened to you in your past is part of the bigger plan.

If you believe something that has happened to you is bad, your reaction to that event will cause you more grief, and the more grief you carry toward that experience, the more grief you will attract into your life. An example of this would be loving parents who have lost a child and still have a child who is living. In so many cases, the extreme grief and grieving over the dead child causes the parents to have more problems in their life and eventually divorce. The child who is alive experiences all the negative aspects in life instead of the parents being grateful for each other and giving more love to each other.

What you believe is your truth. If you believe you are a champion, then you are. If you believe you are a loser, then you are. If you believe you are unlucky and bad things always happen to you, then with the law of attraction, you will bring more of the bad things (or what you consider bad) into your life.

It's time to look at the events that have happened in your life and bless them. Believe that everything that has happened has brought you to where you are today and that you love and approve of yourself right now, in this instant. Changing your belief system toward loving all things past, present, and future will alter the outcomes for you and your success and wellbeing to a more positive state of happiness.

Believe and it shall be. What you believe and the thoughts that surround your belief system will form your reality. Nothing you have done is important, because it is in the past. Nothing you will do is important, because it is in the future. The only important thing is what you do now.

In this book, you will learn how to train your mind toward patterns and habits of thinking that will increase and expand your life experiences. The practice is to pay attention and notice your thoughts. When you notice your habit of dwelling on your problems or thoughts that continue to be negative toward something or someone, all you need to do is be aware of these thoughts and quickly change them to positive thoughts for the outcome you desire.

Habits are just that: habits. Once you become aware of a habitual tendency to think negatively, that habit can easily be changed so that your life is more fulfilling and rewarding. Unconscious, negative thinking happens to all of us when we feel that we were hurt or out of touch with our true selves. Meditation and stillness can help in these circumstances.

When we are still and ask for guidance, the true nature of our inner being will answer. It is always available to guide you to more positive thought patterns and habits of thinking. All is well. Your thoughts create your destiny, so notice the next time a negative thought appears. Bless it for sharing with you and then just let it go.

The full moon has always affected my sleep. Our bodies are made up of 75 percent water, so just like the moon has a gravitational energy with the body of the ocean, the same can happen to the body of a human. Since we are all connected as one within this universe, sensitive people like myself and many others will notice the energy that is transpiring between the moon and our sleep. Instead of feeling agitated or anxious because I am not falling to sleep and it's three a.m., I have made the choice to surround myself with the moon's love and listen to what she may be telling me.

The moon is part of our human world and part of our inherent living. All of the planets have an effect on our lives. Science is proving more and more each day that energy is everything, and everything is connected by energy. Energy cannot be created or destroyed; it just is. When you are exposed to the energy that the full moon is projecting, you have a choice of how to accept it. Accept it with love and thankfulness for the message she is sending to you.

If everything is energy, you can attract the same energy that you are projecting. This is why so many people live with suffering. If parents believe that life is all about suffering and victimhood, then the child is raised to believe the same thing. This becomes a message of energy that will reside in the child's subconscious and be stored there forever. Reprogramming needs to happen so that the child who has grown into an adult can break the pattern.

I experienced this personally when I was growing up. My parents and their parents had a belief that we did not have free will and that God had all the power over us and any of our decisions. I was raised to believe that God was angry and would punish me if I sinned. I would go to a place called hell, and I would burn for eternity. My childish brain believed this for many years, until one day, when I was nineteen, I discovered my truth and decided to listen to my heart and soul instead of the part of my brain where all those negative teachings about the punishing God were stored.

I started questioning everything that I thought and believed and realized that God is love, God is me, and I am God. We are one. I no longer accepted the story of dogma and that God was separate from me. I started reading books on shamanism and Buddhism, and I started living a spiritual life. I started to feel whole and complete instead of fearful and separated. I even started talking to my angels.

There is a hymn from 1921 called "Only Believe." The words are very meditative: "Only believe, only believe, all things are possible, only believe." These words are also a wonderful mantra when you are feeling the day's hectic activities and becoming tired and less than peaceful. You only have to stop for a brief moment, take in a breath, and just repeat the words slowly and with feeling: *only believe.* When I do this, I do truly believe! I believe all things are possible for me and for all people and situations. All I have to do is hold that feeling in my heart, and a peaceful, grateful feeling of joy and exuberance takes over.

My belief that all things are possible, helps me to stay focused and positive. My belief has helped me in so many challenges within my human life. When I was diagnosed with the autoimmune disease called Graves' disease, a hyperthyroid situation where my hormone levels were higher than normal, I was told that I needed to immediately take a radioactive pill that would destroy my thyroid and essentially stop it from producing the high level of hormones. I told the endocrinologist that I needed time to research this decision, as I didn't want to lose my thyroid and take a synthetic pill for the rest of my life.

The doctor said, "I don't believe that it is a good decision, to wait.

You need to get the procedure done sooner, rather than later, since this is a serious disease."

That statement made me think. How many people believe what they are told about their health without doing research or getting a second opinion? How many people believe that there are no other choices? How many people are told they have an autoimmune disease and give up on their health and let fear drive the situation? Fear can fog your decision-making, and fear can give you false beliefs. Only love can heal.

My decision to love myself enough to not immediately take a radioactive pill was the best decision I could have made. My belief that my body is intelligent and my body loves me just as much as I love it was the first step in my healing. I read everything about Graves' disease, but I read it without fear. I met a doctor who agreed that balancing my thyroid with acupuncture, supplements, and food would help my body get back to a normal production of thyroid hormones. All I needed to do was to support these activities with my belief that I could heal.

Because I had healed myself from esophagitis twenty-five years before, I truly believed that I could heal myself of this diagnosis of Graves' disease. Of course, the first thing I started doing was using Louise Hay affirmations for hyperthyroid: "I am at the center of life, and I approve of myself and all that I see." I said that affirmation hundreds of times a day. I sang it while exercising, while preparing the healthy food for my thyroid, and also while I was on the table with acupuncture needles that were helping my body. I repeated the affirmation and added, "Only believe, only believe, all things are possible, only believe."

As I opened myself up to receiving the healing I needed, a book popped up on my Facebook page called *Thyroid Healing: The Truth behind Graves' Disease* by Anthony William. This book was truly a godsend (I like that word), because I knew the universe was supporting my belief that I could heal myself. The book said this: "Soon, you'll understand the reality of what's going on with your thyroid, and the rest of your body, and you'll be able to use that truth to help yourself heal." That quote was a prophecy, and that prophecy came true for me within a year of reading it. I believed it with all my heart, and with that truth, along with balancing my body with acupuncture, eating the right foods for my health, and repeating my mantras for healing, I can stand here today and tell you that I do not have Graves' disease or any of its symptoms.

I have also been a perfect example to others. I lead them to the book *Thyroid Healing* and to the trust and belief that they can heal. As Anthony William predicted, "You will contribute to a true healing movement. Your experience will help so many, more than you'll ever know." I tell you, this has happened on so many occasions. At the grocery store, at the bookstore, online, or among friends and family, I have been able to lead others to thyroid truth.

My belief that I can choose my thoughts, my belief that I am a powerful machine that can be repaired, and my belief that all things are possible is a stronghold in my life. I have peace and purpose in my life. I am balanced.

Here is another way that a belief system worked in a controlled setting. Duke University had a project named Project Mantra. It consisted of working with people who'd recently had surgery. Half of the people were prayed for every day, and the other half were not prayed for. Researchers discovered that the people who were prayed for had fewer side effects and healed faster than the ones not prayed for. The people praying had a strong belief in what they were doing and a belief that we are all connected. This is a great example of how we can heal ourselves as well as help to heal others.

Our beliefs are our truth. So, we need to know our own truths and make sure they are not false beliefs or programs in our subconscious that are causing us to be separate from our most authentic selves. When we reach this true state and awareness in our consciousness, true healing can take place. When you align with the universe, there are no impossibilities. Believing and trusting in your authentic self is a gift you can share with others to help them heal. You just have to uncover the truth. And as we have heard throughout our lives, "The truth shall set you free."

Andrew Newberg, MD, and Mark Waldman are world-renowned for their neuroscientific research on spirituality and consciousness. They say that "in neuroscience and in many other fields, there's rarely enough evidence to prove anything. The brain is rarely interested in proof. It's interested in results: pleasure, goal achievement, satisfaction, curiosity, problem solving and fun."

The dictionary also suggests that trust, faith, and confidence are needed to sustain a strong belief. We ask ourselves then, do the same neuroscientific rules apply to religion? By definition, a belief is "the acceptance that a statement is true or that something exists in reality." But there are so many belief systems with regard to religion. Many religions have been formed based on personal experience and also on what other religious authorities say.

So the question arises: "Which one do you choose to believe and why?" Newberg and Waldman say that spirituality instead of religion reflects a neuroscientific ideal: if you train your mind and brain to not believe in one single spiritual truth or one specific definition of a reality or God, your mind, brain, and heart can judge less and be more open toward the acceptance of others who hold dramatically different beliefs or disbeliefs.

This type of living, for me personally, has allowed for less judging and more love toward others. It is my way of learning and listening and being objective, because I now realize that we are all on our own spiritual or religious journey. It is not up to me to change other people's beliefs or realities, because it is their life, not mine. What I can do is love and try to be more compassionate, which sends out positive energy. My inner being in balance is my true authentic self. Others will be attracted to me to learn more, and trust more, by seeing my life as an example of true happiness and joy.

I do not have the power to change anyone else's beliefs; only they have that personal power, and I will not tell them they are right or wrong. I can just be my authentic self so that others don't feel small around me. I give them the opportunity to feel my energy so the trust is there for them to believe in me. I do not have any ultimatums, just love.

Newberg and Waldman have a little game I have played with my mind that I find very effective when I practice, no judgment. Try it out: Assume there are no facts, no proof and no truth. Assume everything you see and feel is an imaginary concept you've taken for granted for many years. Assume it is not true. How does that feel? What happens to your most sacred beliefs, and how does that affect your view of reality?

When I do this mind game often, I can get a small glimpse of a neurological state of enlightenment where old beliefs dissolve and I can experience myself aligning with the universe in a brand new, exciting way. I can let others believe the way they want with no judgment, hate, or thinking they are wrong. I need only be who I am and what I believe.

Your beliefs can and will form your personality. Have you ever asked yourself, "Where does my personality come from?" There are many assessment tests you can take to assign a certain personality label to yourself, but you will also find that if you take it again on a different day, your emotions play a big part in helping you to get different results. When we are angry, a different personality emerges; when we are joyful, a different personality will show up. So, ask yourself: *What personality do I want to have?*

Behavior is born from many different things: your life experiences, your environment, and most of all, your belief system. Albert Einstein has a famous question that he asked a group of scientist colleagues: "Is the world a friendly place?" The scientists spoke on this topic for days as they disagreed that the world is or isn't friendly. What they could all agree on was, "Whatever you think, then it is."

If you believe there is no way to be successful, then your mind and subconscious will also believe it. What you give out, you will receive. What you think about comes about. If you believe that you are happy, you will receive or bring more things into your life to be happy about. Your life today is the result of a series of decisions you made that have caused you to arrive where you are. All the little decisions compound over time to give results that will cause you to be successful or to fail.

Believing and Feeling

Realize the frequency that you are on and in with your feelings. You must feel the positive manifestation. Not just words can make things happen. The feeling is the way to source. Having the feeling of alignment will continue to bring more alignment. Having misaligned thoughts can cause dis-ease, and practicing the negative feelings you are attracting will only continue to bring those misaligned thoughts.

Influence, integrity, and inspiration are all inner feelings of alignment. These are all truths, not lies. Having the feeling of joy that inspires or influences is pure creativity and direct alignment. What feels good is your clue as to what the higher source wants for you. Source is always there—the support from source feelings—and when you don't resist those feelings from source, it will provide clarity regarding what you really want.

Absence of love is fear. When you can release the fear, then there will be more love. When you are tuned in to love, you are like a light that attracts more love. You cannot serve others until you serve yourself and let go of fear. Be happy and be more balanced. When you look for something to fill the void and continue to feel empty, that means you are not in the frequency of your perfect alignment. This is a clue to you to make a change.

How do you change? You must ask yourself why: *Why do I feel a void?* Asking the *why* will help you to determine what you don't want and foster what you do want. If you are continuing to feel discomfort, disagreement, and disease, you are not in a state of allowing. You are in a state of resisting. You have to find a way to believe in what you want.

Steve Jobs and Bill Gates knew what they wanted and believed it was possible. I started believing that I could be a speaker and workshop leader, and before I knew it, I was interviewing with a real estate brokerage that wanted me to lead workshops and classes on my own success. You must be in your highest consciousness to believe and then take action.

There is no need to continue to suffer. Everyone has choices, and everyone has the opportunity to change. When you tune in to your true desire, you will not continue to suffer. You will find happiness. It only takes the will to feel it—free will.

We are creators of our own destiny. Why do you choose to do things out of fear instead of out of love? Why do we sometimes make choices easily and quickly from our own feelings and intuitions brought about from trust and joy?

Inspiration always creates positive manifestation, and we all have it. We just need to find out what inspires us. What do you want to create and why? If you know the *why*, it will help you to discover what you need to do. You will start believe in yourself and, in turn, be inspired to create.

You should try to be the best possible version of yourself. Do you trust yourself? If not, again, ask *why*. I know what it feels like to not trust yourself, and I now believe in my purpose. I am open to believing that everything that brings me desire and joy will come into my life.

Now try this: Close your eyes and imagine the best possible version of yourself. Take a few minutes to see it as clearly as possible. That's the real you! That is who you really are. So now, you can let go of any of the *you* that doesn't believe it. The only way we can grow is by doing things that we are uncomfortable with at first. We will learn from mistakes and use those feelings to grow. Become aware of what makes you uncomfortable or afraid. These are the feelings you need to trust the most.

Life is too short to spend another day at war with yourself. Learn to love and believe in yourself every day. Why are so many of us at war with ourselves? Don't you feel that is bizarre? Perhaps it is about feeling depressed or slighted when we were young by the words, actions, or omissions of others. When did we take on this feeling about ourselves? And why? Ask yourself this question, and that is the first step.

It is time to discover your true self and say "no more" to self-deprecating thoughts, no more to low self-esteem. Quit the self-hatred and ask for self-love. Declare peace. It is between you and yourself. Only you can bring peace to yourself.

Let go of negative thoughts that come when you are trying something new. Is it really that scary? Praise yourself for even trying. When you fail at something, try, try again. Having a friend, family member, coach, or therapist can help change your thoughts with encouragement and support to learn to love yourself without diminishing thoughts. It is difficult, but possible. Ask peace to surround you, penetrate you, and inhabit every aspect of your being.

Ask to be the best possible version of yourself. Believe you are that person. How does it feel? Know it and trust that it is you. Just believe.

When we are born, there is only love. But growing up as a child, we learn about hate, disappointment, negative thoughts, and, essentially, fear. Fear is the absence of love. We must switch our thoughts of fear and negativity to ask the question, "How may I serve today?" How can you make someone else's day? Get rid of the thoughts of only what you want and desire. Ask how you can be of service. Once you determine the value you can offer, you will find value in yourself, and love will erase fear.

What you focus on will come into your life. What you focus on expands and will become a part of your reality. The outside world is a reflection of your inner life. So you should ask yourself: how is your inner life?

Do you worry about your finances? How are your relationships with friends and loved ones? What about your health? Are you happy with your career? When you ask yourself these questions, you must start with reestablishing who you are, your identity, and just return to the basics to see how you can make changes. The changes must happen first within yourself in order to see changes outside yourself.

You must realize that you are made of love. You are whole. You are perfect. When you begin to think these thoughts consciously, your life will reflect the same back to you. These are some of the lessons taught by Louise Hay. I became a "Heal Your Life" workshop leader in 2016 in order to practice these techniques and belief habits. You must affirm it and really, really believe that it takes place in order to have the best results. If you are looking for this evidence outside of yourself, to create a fuller life, then you are missing the point. The evidence is not outside of you, it is inside of you.

What are your feelings or beliefs about yourself? Do this exercise now: List ten things that you criticize about yourself. Now look at the list with love. Can you just love yourself and say, "I believe in myself, and I am doing best that I can do." Now doesn't that feel better? Remember this: your thoughts about yourself and the feelings you have about the state of your life are actually more important than what other people think about you. Take some time, sit, and listen to your inner dialogue about yourself. When you look at your list of your feelings about yourself, can you see that what you are thinking about tends to show up in your life?

Now, do this new exercise and write down ten things that you think people feel about you. Are they the same? Are they more positive? Sometimes what we think people think of us we make our reality—and again, we are making their perception of us the truth.

When I was in junior high school, I was an overachiever. I was on the gymnastic team, cheerleading squad, track team, and dive team. I was an A-plus student and a class officer. I played guitar, sang in church choir, and raised money for MS. I was so busy that I was running from activity to activity.

One day, I heard someone talking negatively about me, saying, "She is so stuck up!" and "Monica is so in love with herself!" I became very upset about these comments. They made me angry. How could it be so wrong or negative to love yourself?

I spoke with my counselor and told her my feelings. I was thirteen years old, and I felt that everything I was doing was not worth doing if people saw me like this. She was so wise, and I will never forget her words: "Monica, people will talk about you until you are six feet under. Their perception of you might be their reality, but it's what you think of yourself that truly matters."

At thirteen, girls are very impressionable. I needed to listen to how I felt about myself, take time to smile at people, ask how they were doing, and be more involved with others instead of rushing around doing all my activities. I slowly realized that I was doing a lot of those activities because I wanted people to think great things about me. Once I started to do things for myself and to make *me* happy, I did not care what others thought about my desires and dreams. I would continue to love myself and not feel shame for it.

I wanted to be the best person I could be. Soon I noticed that the girls who made the comments about me were starting to see that I was caring, was a good listener, and just loved who I was. I was happy with my life. Soon, positive things came from this event of people talking negatively about me.

I learned two things that day:

1. I am perfect just the way I am.
2. Others' perception of me is not my reality.

I needed to learn that it was okay to love myself and to want the best for myself. I gained this insight at a young age. It is easy. Once we change the negative thoughts of ourselves and others into loving positive thoughts, there will be a shift, and our life together on this planet will change.

All that we are is a result of what we have thought. The mind is everything. What we think, we become.—Buddha

CHAPTER 2

Allowing

*The principle of cause and effect is the truth
that allows us to better ourselves and the
world around us. Madisyn Taylor*

llowing is the path of least resistance. Open yourself and your mind to receiving the best. The law of receptivity is, "In order to receive good, we must expect good and also give good to others." This means allowing yourself to receive all that is already seeking you in return.

Have you ever wondered why some people seem lucky while others have bad things happen more often than good? This is an example of the cause and effect theory. If you have no resistance to life and have an intention to and awareness of what you want, good things will follow. The same happens when you put up resistance to life. If you think the world is an unfriendly place, then it is. Your awareness of allowing life to happen and being open to receiving all that is good will cause positive things to happen for you.

However, sometimes when change is happening and we don't necessarily know that change is taking place, universal law is actually at work as a form of energy. Our own energy, which is universal energy, can be affecting not only the people we see and interact with every day but also billions of people around the world that we may never meet. Allowing your intentions to influence your decisions and the way you speak and feel has an effect on all that there is in this world.

I know it sounds illogical, but the law of cause and effect is happening every second of our lives. So ask yourself: *Am I an influencer of good and positive outcomes, or am I an influencer of negative outcomes?*

Our influence is endless; it is infinite. It is hard to fathom that our thoughts and actions can affect our jobs, our relationships, and our own lives, much less billions of people and situations around the world. We just need to allow our conscience to guide us because that is the truest and most authentic way to be of service to mankind, as well as our planet earth that we call home. When you allow and listen to your most authentic inner being, you will have less chaos, more harmony, and more balance. The more balance you have in your life, the more you will be influencing the world of positivity. The effect is a positive one that can help alter the negative energy that is being influenced by others.

When you throw a stone in a pond, the ripple that expands is from that little rock. In the same way, everything you do and feel is rippling out to the world. All of the thoughts and actions we take may have an effect on others and the earth that we can't even comprehend. If you allow your awareness of the little things that are thoughts to be transformed by your positive intentions, and always promote peace, love, and compassion for yourself as well as others, your influences in this world will always be considered miracles. From the day we are born to the day we die, we have a choice to be a positive influence or a negative one. It is up to us how we want the universal energy to play out.

From a spiritual perspective, you can imagine that light is allowing and darkness is disallowing. If you live your life in the light, so to speak, then light will surround you and draw more light to you. You will find that you will have less stress and more positivity, because light overcomes darkness in all situations.

Try this exercise: Sit in a completely dark room, light a small candle, and watch how the light takes over and eventually lights the entire room. Your thinking can work the same way. If you are having negative thoughts or worries that cloud or darken your attitude, all you need to do to switch your thoughts to light is be grateful. Being grateful is the candle that will take over and light the entire room (of your mind) and stamp out the darkness. When you switch your attitude, you allow yourself to accept all the good that is already there waiting for you to enjoy it.

Allow is a funny-looking word. When you break it into two words, it looks like *all* and *ow*. Like accepting it *all* can sometimes feel like an *ow*. What I have learned from life is that we can have it all, but it can be painful if we don't slow down and enjoy having it all. Allow yourself to not only be open to receiving the abundance that is *all* readily available to you, but also allow yourself the time and the stillness to be thankful for the abundance, joy, and love that you are receiving.

The Latin word for *allow* is *sino*. *Sino* is defined as "suffer, permit, or let." *Allow* in Latin also has other meanings, like "to concede." When you allow or concede or, in other words, give up, what happens is you become open to the good that is there for you to accept—no forcing it to happen, no stress to make it happen, and no disappointment when things just don't turn out the way you so desperately want them to. It's called the path of least resistance or the path of allowing.

Abraham Hicks, an entity who speaks through Ester Hicks, describes this as the experience that we need to realize is the first step to getting what we are really meant to have. Ester says we are source beings, and when you ask, "it is given." The problem arises when you start to ask for things and try to make things happen that are not reflective of your true path. You may not be paying attention and allow the conditions of your surroundings to drive your life. Then you become stressed because you are putting up resistance to things that are really supposed to be a part of your life. You have a momentum of asking, then getting, then having thoughts or vibrations of feeling that it is not enough, then conditions of not enough will start to happen.

The path of least resistance is the true path. You must find your true reaction to the feelings inside. Does it feel like there is still a void? What is really happening is the feeling that there is just never enough.

If you start to practice the art of gratitude and allow gratitude to open your heart to thoughts of prosperity and clarification that what you are projecting is that you *do* have enough joy in everything you do, you can plan for the abundance to be aligned with your needs and desires. But if you are not balanced with your thoughts, you will find that you are putting up resistance to the things you really want out of life instead of allowing them to come to you.

For example, consider the *buts* in your goal of weight loss, finding a soul mate, earning more money. *But if only I could lose weight, then I would be happy. But if only I could find my soul mate, then I could be happy.* Get rid of the *buts*—no excuses.

Decreasing work and increasing freedom is the art of allowing—for example, allowing yourself to see that you can work less but still have an increase in income. This happens because you are open to allowing yourself to take vacations with family, to take care of clients, and to do all this without feeling guilty.

Surrender is a form of allowing. *Surrender,* to me, actually means to come over to the winning side. Surrendering doesn't have to mean "weak." True surrender takes courage. Surrender to the fact that something isn't working for you.

There comes a day when you will need to surrender to change—and to realize that change is a better way. You are the creator of the conditions in your life, the ones you are proud of and the ones you wish never happened. By surrendering to this, you will actually be putting yourself in the seat of power, where you belong, with full authority over your life. When you change your thinking about something you have done or something you wish had not happened, allow yourself to change your thinking about it to accommodate a new idea.

Say this to yourself: "I am not the conditions of my life. I am the creator of those conditions, so I have the power to make new ones. I believe that life is constantly testing me for my level of commitment. I deserve the rewards that life has to offer, and I will demonstrate a never-ending commitment to act until I achieve."

I have had many experiences of opening and allowing spiritual things to happen to me. For example, I had a friend who overdosed one night. I found out via a long-distance phone call from his mother. She told me that he was in the hospital and had taken too much LSD, and he was coming in and out of consciousness. I began to pray to the Archangel Raphael, the angel of healing. I was on my knees at three in the morning praying that the archangel would help my friend and save him from dying.

That night, as I lay crying and praying, Archangel Raphael showed himself to me. I was awakened by an intensely bright light in the vanity area of my bathroom. The mirrors intensified the light, but I was able to see the large figure of an angel. He was so tall that his back was leaning over and his wings were layered flat on his back. I felt scared, and I gasped. In that same moment, he disappeared. All of a sudden, I felt peace, and I was able to sleep. After that, I had a feeling my friend was now okay.

I woke in the morning to find out my friend had survived but had been dead for a few minutes. He told me that an angel visited with him, and that he was shown something and given a feeling that he needed to be alive. I did not tell him about my visit with Archangel Raphael, because I didn't want to sound crazy.

For three days, I waited to tell my husband about that strange visitor in our bathroom. When I finally told him, I felt like I was losing my mind and that I must be going crazy. But my husband said he believed me. At that moment, I realized that I had the power to ask for someone to be healed or for myself to be healed. I understood that I could trust that my prayers are really answered. All I had to do was believe and then be open to allowing the prayer to be answered.

> *The answer does not lie in any personal ability we may have or may not have... but in contacting the infinite storehouse within.—Joel Goldsmith.*

Forgiving as a Form of Allowing

The best spiritual practice for your inner-being balance is forgiveness. It is one of the most important spiritual wisdoms that can assist us in keeping our divine connection with the universe open and clear. It can also be the most difficult. But if we can learn to go into our inner selves and into our quiet minds, we can release the burden to the infinite and also ask for assistance to forgive. When you learn to forgive, more freedom will come into your life. You will see that letting go of that real or imagined hurt will release your mind and heart from bondage.

Forgiveness of yourself can be very difficult. There may be something you are embarrassed that you have done, or you may carry guilt over something from the past. You must remember that it is the past, and the past no longer exists, so in releasing and forgiving yourself, you can move forward without that burden or shame.

Forgiveness will allow a better and brighter present. You can be free at any moment from years of self-doubt or years of hating someone if you only release it to the universe. Forgiveness allows us to know that the universe holds nothing against us, as we learn to hold nothing against ourselves.

From the age of three until I was five, I was sexually abused by a close family member. It was not every night, or even very often, but it occurred on several occasions when I was left in this person's care at his home.

What I remember most about these events was seeing the clock, which had glow-in-the-dark flip numbers. When it would flip to 11:11, I felt an overwhelming sense of peace that all would be okay. I know that I was half asleep when this abuse took place, and I do not remember any pain. I do not believe that any type of rape or intercourse took place on those evenings. But the older I became, the more I believed that what he was doing was not a good thing, especially when he told me not to tell my parents.

I think this is where my innocence was stolen and I started to believe that it was okay to lie and okay to keep secrets from my parents. I prayed that it would stop and that it would never happen to my sisters. My prayers were answered when my dad announced that he was being transferred and we were moving two hours away from our city. I truly believe that this was my first occurrence of wishing and focusing on something that I really wanted in my life and manifesting it to happen.

Once we moved away to a new life, away from my abuser, I started over. I consciously decided that I would block out all those memories from my mind. But I would still see 11:11 as a sign that all was okay in my life. I would never attach that sign to what happened to me in the past. It was the beginning of my 11:11 future.

What I discovered from therapy many years later, is that I formed a relationship with that symbol because of a feeling I had at such a young age. This feeling helped me to cope. This feeling helped me to believe that I had angels around me and that I could call upon them to protect me.

Many years went by. I was working in New York when I met a woman who told me of her experiences with incest as a child. I had not thought of the sexual abuse at all for more than ten years, but the subconscious part of our brain holds everything in the past forever. All the visions and feelings of fear came back to my mind.

I told my husband, my parents, and my sisters. I felt it was very hard for them to hear. The memories were difficult to share, and it made me feel unworthy and shameful. That's when I decided that I needed therapy to help me with the disturbing thoughts.

I went through a method of learning to love my inner child. I was shown how to heal from past trauma by holding an image of myself as a child and hugging my past self and telling her I loved her. It was amazing, and I still use this inner child therapy when I have memories come up from that time in my childhood. I have also forgiven my abuser.

I feel no shame in telling you this story. I am a proud woman with no shame of my past. What has also helped me heal is my belief that 11:11 was symbolic of a good feeling instead of a bad thing that happened to me. We all have a choice as to what we want to believe. I believe that the sign of 11:11 will forever hold a positive feeling rather than a negative one.

I allow myself to see that whatever happened to me in the past is over and done. I live in the now, and I am blessed. When 11:11 shows up for me even now, I take a deep breath, smile, and move along, knowing that my inner guidance is at work for me always.

By allowing myself to be open to the sign of 11:11 having an authentic symbolization for me, I discovered that I am not the only person to have that connection. There is an 1111 radio show, an 1111 magazine, 1111 books, 1111 memberships, and 1111 websites. I connected with an Indian chief from a Lakota tribe in South Dakota. He was traveling the nation holding drum circles and meditations on 1111 when he stopped in my small town of Golden, Colorado, for one of his 1111 events. Knowing that so many people have the same meaningful relationship to the symbolization 1111 helps me to affirm that I am not alone.

What is your sign or symbol? Some people like to have a spirit animal that may show up in their life or in their mediations. Be open to allowing and learning what spirit animal, insect, reptile, or bird connects with you and allow it to connect to your inner being and guide you to answers or paths that you are searching for.

I discovered my spirit animal about twenty-four years ago when I was camping in the mountains of Georgia. It was a Cherokee Indian reservation and eco-village. You could rent a teepee or a cabin, and they had gardens and beautiful hikes around the area.

There was a Cherokee wedding that my husband, my three-year-old, and myself got to view. The bride and groom each had a wolf standing beside them during the ceremony. It was an amazing and very special moment in my life to see this ceremony transpire.

After we watched the wedding, we walked around the village. As we passed a sweat lodge, there was an old Indian woman sitting outside, and she summoned me to come speak with her. At first, I was a little skeptical, due to past programming in my subconscious, but then I just allowed myself to walk over and see what she had to say. She was very old, with layers and layers of wrinkles, and she had two long gray braids that went past her waist. She sat there whittling a small piece of wood and chewing tobacco.

I immediately felt her love and energy and was not afraid. She told me that she felt my energy as I walked past her and that I should join the wedding party in a sweat lodge that would be happening in a few minutes. I had always wanted to participate in a Native American sweat lodge ceremony, so I of course said yes. She looked at my husband and son and told them it was only for me.

My husband and son left to go back to our cabin. She continued by explaining to me how the sweat lodge worked. I needed to ask a question of the higher power (God, universe) called Unahlahnauhi and set an intention or prayer for an answer. If I had something on me to symbolize my question or situation, then I should bury it outside in mother earth.

My dilemma back then was that I felt unbalanced in my job life and my family life. I was working all the time and flying all over the nation for my job in the fashion industry, and I had very little time to spend with my firstborn child and husband. I had a picture in my wallet of all three of us, so I took that out, and as I buried it, I asked the higher power and also mother earth to help me receive answers on how I could balance my work and life. I buried the picture and then went into the sweat lodge.

I was the only Caucasian person there; everyone else was a Cherokee. I felt so privileged in that moment to be invited to share this ceremony that tribes had performed for centuries. I allowed myself to just relax and learn. It was pitch black inside, and you could only hear the old woman chant and drum.

The fire keeper opened the layers of fur pelts over the entrance and added hot stones from the fire to the middle of the lodge. Then he closed the entrance back down. The old woman added water to the hot rocks, and we experienced a wave of hot air and humidity. At first, I was afraid, since I felt it was so hot, and how could I stay in there for very long? But as the chanting and drumming continued, I started to feel the rhythm with my heartbeat, and I began to relax.

The old woman had warned me earlier, before entering, that they planned to stay for five or six hours in the lodge. If I felt I needed to leave, I would have to leave mother earth's womb (the sweat lodge) breach, by going out the entrance backward. I agreed.

As I lay there inside mother nature's womb, I contemplated the question of how to balance work and life. I eventually fell into a trance or dreamworld, as they called it. A female wolf entered my dream, and she had baby wolf pups. I felt the wolf's love and care for her pups. I could feel that the spirit of this amazing creature was in me, and we were one. I can still feel this feeling of oneness to this day when I visualize the wolf during my meditations.

The crazy thing that happened next was I woke very abruptly, and a feeling came over me that my husband and child needed me right then. I proceeded to crawl toward the entrance/exit of the sweat lodge. By sheer circumstance, the fire keeper knew that he needed to open the layers of fur pelts and allow me to crawl backward out into the real world. I didn't know until later that I had been in the sweat lodge for three hours.

I ran very fast back to our cabin, and there I found my husband vomiting into the toilet and my three-year-old screaming and crying. I immediately picked up my son and went to help my husband. He said that they took a long hike up to a waterfall and that he had drank the water. Within a few hours, he was throwing up from it. I felt this amazing power come over me as he told me he was wishing that I would come help him.

I told him about my intentional prayer and the sweat lodge, and we both realized at that moment that we had a special bond. Whenever we needed each other, we would be able to connect to that energy and seek each other out, no matter where we were. My answer to my question in the sweat lodge was to follow my intuition and listen to my inner being for balance.

I have claimed the female wolf as my spirit animal, and I can at any time seek answers while meditating with her. Just like a mother wolf, who can sense danger to her family, I can sense this in my own life. It has been miraculous, to say the least. Looking for signs in life and having trust they mean something is an important way to allow good things to happen to you.

Getting back to forgiveness, many people feel that the act of an adult taking advantage of a young innocent child is unforgivable. But I tell you, I did not fully heal until the day I released the anger and forgave my abuser. I was able to release the embarrassment, release the shame, and realize that it was not something I had asked to happen to me. It was part of my past that I no longer had to give any energy to. I was okay.

Forgiveness isn't easy, but it isn't impossible, either. There were times in my life when I felt I could never forgive my abuser. How do you get to the point where you feel that it is possible to forgive? No matter how horrible the act, believe me when I say it can be done.

Why is it so important to forgive? Forgiveness provides freedom. Forgiveness of someone who has hurt you physically or has betrayed you can actually help you to move past the hurt. Dwelling on the act in your mind can become a burden of anger and resentment. It can harden your heart. You should not just block it from your mind, but talk about it, name it, and then release it to the past. Then you can begin to renew your heart and soul and accept that you are free from the past hurt. Forgiveness opens your mind and spirit to allowing—allowing love instead of hate.

Do this exercise: Close your eyes and take a deep breath. Is there anyone you want to forgive? Is there someone you feel you can forgive right now? Bring that person or people into your mind right now with your eyes shut. See them with light surrounding them and either say out loud or in your mind, "I forgive you." Then release them into that light and take some more deep breaths before you open your eyes. You should feel lighter and freer now. If the anger or resentment comes back, just remember this exercise and forgive them again until you no longer feel that the act they did deserves any more of your time or energy. Now you are truly free.

If I told you that the pain of being wronged doesn't have to hurt so much, would you believe me? Maybe not. But would you *like* to believe me? I can say that once I forgive anyone who I feel has wronged me, I feel more powerful in the situation. Forgiveness can make you powerful because it frees you from what other people do and have done.

I truly believe that forgiveness is a gift you give to yourself. It's true that forgiveness isn't always easy to do, but it is possible when you think about it differently. You don't need to force it, just release it day by day until you allow the act of forgiveness to open your heart. Forgiveness is an act of grace, and grace can only flow into an open heart.

Releasing and realigning are part of allowing. You can release thoughts that hold you down or thoughts that are of blame, and then your inner being can realign with the universe.

Let the Universe Be Your Guide

How can you be guided by the universe? Think about when you are planning something. You can allow your inner wisdom to guide you. Your inner wisdom is your GPS for your highest self. Think of it like this: the light from your inner wisdom can shine like a beacon to guide you to the answers you are asking about in your life plan or your life journey. No matter how big the decision, your inner wisdom can help you make the wisest choices if you allow it to.

Whenever I feel undecided or insecure about the direction I should take, I allow my inner guide to take over. I know that my underlying intelligence will guide me to my greatest good. When you trust yourself and trust the universe, you will be perfectly aligned and balanced, and then you can tune in and allow the next steps to be presented to you. This happens when you practice living in the moment. Your intuition is your inner guide, and you can be at peace with your decisions.

Here is a great example of trusting that the universe has got your back. I had a miscarriage two years after I had already given birth to my firstborn son. I was almost five months pregnant, so I went to the doctor for the ultrasound to check on everything and find out the sex of this baby who I loved, growing inside of me. When the ultrasound showed that the baby girl had died, my first emotion was denial. The next was anger, and the third was sadness.

I sat in my car with my perfectly healthy two-year-old boy, and I allowed myself to let go and just let God. I allowed my inner wisdom to help me see that all was still well in my world. Yes, this moment was truly sad, but as I considered my appreciation for having a healthy two-year-old, the insight I gained in that moment was that this child inside my stomach was not ready for this world. Nature had taken care of that baby and me.

I began to realize that I had an important decision to make. I could either feel like a victim, have a mindset of scarcity, and ask why did this happen to me, or I could be grateful that nature had taken its course and be grateful for knowing that I could plan to have another child. That child would be healthy, like the child I was looking at right in that moment. This was my firstborn, who was two years old and very healthy.

I allowed my inner wisdom to fill me with love and joy and abundance. I let it guide me to the decision that I could get pregnant again, and I would give birth at another time in the future. My inner guide was correct, and the trust that I put in that decision in that precise moment allowed me to be joyful and compassionate instead of upset and angry. I gave birth to another healthy baby boy two years later.

The art of allowing can put you in a place of growth. As you open yourself up to the path of least resistance, your world will also open up to more opportunities.

I started the practice of allowing at a young age. I was thirteen when I decided to start taking computer courses, since I had a gut feeling that computers were the future. Mind you, it was 1977, and very few people even knew what a computer was. I had heard that in my small town of Conyers, Georgia, there was a new high school being built, and it would have courses for learning about computers and computer science. My intuitive nature and the art of allowing prompted my mind to ask questions about how I could attend that high school instead of the high school that was geographically set for my attendance, and that all my sisters and brothers attended. I had no doubt that I could make this possible, even though our home was on the other side of the railroad tracks where the less fortunate lived.

I felt in my heart and soul that if I applied for that school, and my mom drove me and picked me up, they would allow me to attend. Well, it happened, and everything I wished and prayed for was granted. I was the only kid out of seven kids in my family to attend this modern school that would have computers and computer courses.

Those four years allowed me to learn everything I needed to expand my future in college, where I majored in computer science. Still practicing the art of allowing and knowing in my heart, I could create anything I desired for my future. I was walking past an office after leaving a meeting with my counselor when I saw a flyer posted on the door that said "IBM is interviewing and hiring co-op students."

I had no idea what a co-op student was, but I had definitely heard of IBM. My self-confidence and my knowing allowed me to knock on that door of opportunity (literally). I asked the gentleman inside what was the co-op program and if I could interview. He nicely said back to me that IBM would hire students to work a quarter and then attend college a quarter. I announced enthusiastically that this program was perfect for me. I needed money for college as well as a job.

He politely asked what level of school I was. I said freshman, and he replied, "Sorry, this program is for juniors only, and you must have a 3.5 GPA or better."

I didn't frown or flinch at his response. I just politely told him that I had a grade point average of 3.75 and that I had already taken four years of computer science in high school. I continued by saying I would love to interview with him even though I was a freshman, and maybe he could reconsider.

I got the job! I was eighteen and working for a major corporation like IBM. By allowing myself to believe in myself and open myself to all opportunities, I used the law of attraction, the law of value, and the law of compensation to attract the right person to me for my future.

We can also learn from the things we are resistant to. Becoming aware of why you are resisting something is a wonderful way to grow. To become free and have an inner being in balance is to acknowledge that resistance. Once you do this, ask yourself why. Is it fear? What are you afraid of? Is there something you can change to release some of the doubt and worry? Can you forgive yourself and this situation so that your heart is open with less resistance?

The greatest things in life do not come to us through our intellect; they are experienced in the heart. Allow yourself to feel, to experience, to love, and to appreciate all that is good in this world. Think of how spectacular nature is and how wonderful life is. Open your eyes, open your heart, and allow yourself to receive the gifts that are waiting for you. We live in an amazing, complex, and giving universe. Allow yourself to bask in the goodness with infinite ways to be creative. The universe is your playground, so don't be afraid to soar! Be willing to receive the blessings of the universe and celebrate every moment you are alive.

We all have potential to allow the best version of ourselves to emerge. Just feel how big you can feel by allowing all the best to come to you, all the joy you allow yourself to receive, all the joy you can give by allowing less resistance to pain, uncertainty, and unforgiveness. Forgive yourself for even thinking that you don't deserve the best that life has to offer. When you start allowing good to come to you, you are aligning with your most authentic self. Your inner being will find true balance, and you can manifest the life of your dreams.

The greatest gift you can give to someone is allowing them to be themselves without any judgment. They have their own inner beings, and they are on their own path. So, when you are in a relationship and you want someone to agree with you, instead of trying to make them be something that they are not, just allow them to discover things about themselves. Expectations and conditions are putting a conditional love and conditional expectations on the relationship.

You can say this: "I love you so much. I'm willing to listen, and I don't have to judge you. Since my inner being is different from yours, I accept you, if you can accept me."

What if someone you love is suffering? You can let your inner being guide you and direct you to listen and help without judging. Just ask, "What can I do to help? Know that feeling my love for you can help you to love yourself."

What about negative people in your life? Just learn to mediate on them. Let what you are observing have more of a neutral tone and don't judge them, as they have their own inner being that might not be on the same level or frequency as yours. You can thank them for their opinion, thank them for caring, and just let the energy of love clear it up. They don't have to change to agree with you. They may not ever change, so you can just not care or give it negative power.

The coolest thing about letting your inner being be your guide and no one else's, is that your inner being knows what you desire and also knows how to get there. You just have to allow it. Allowing the universe or your higher self to lead the way is called "cause and effect." When you spend time in meditation each day (the cause), your mind will feel peace and balance (the effect). When you love yourself (the cause), you will be loved by others (the effect). When you live your life on purpose (the cause), your life will have meaning (the effect). When you give (the cause), then so you will receive (the effect).

That is why it is so important to give your best, so that you will receive the best back. When you celebrate who you are by allowing all the good to manifest for yourself, you are feasting on life, with love as the center of it all.

Be thankful for what you have; you'll end up having more. If you concentrate on what you don't have, you will never, ever have enough.—*Oprah Winfrey*

The universe, in its natural state, is always providing in abundance. There is always enough. When we allow ourselves to be aware of this natural flow of abundance, we are aligning ourselves with the abundant flow of life. When you appreciate the things in life that you already have, this flow and alignment with the universe releases the barriers you may have set up regarding lack. Being in a state of appreciation, is allowing abundance to be the focus instead of focusing on what you don't have.

That's how the universe works. What you focus on expands, so when you focus on and appreciate what you do have, you will receive more of it. This is the law of receptivity. When you focus on things you don't have, as in the Oprah quote, your focus on lack will only bring you more lack. This is the law of attraction. By opening up and allowing abundance to vibrate with you through the art of gratitude, you are aligning yourself with the universe in the most natural state of always having enough. We will talk more about expanding in a later chapter.

I have a great story about using appreciation as a stepping-stone to allowing good to come into my life. I call it "Bankruptcy and Blame, Worry and Shame: How I Changed My Thoughts and Gave Thanks for Bankruptcy." The universe opened up, and there arose all kinds of opportunity for me to teach. I became a foreclosure intervention specialist. I helped people who were facing the same stress that I had faced and helped them to avoid bankruptcy and foreclosure. I turned a situation that happened in my life into a positive.

If I had never faced this situation in my own life, I would not have had that experience to share with others. I allowed my positive feelings around the so-called negative experience to change the way I felt about it, and I was able to help others.

Balancing Your Brain

In their book *NeuroWisdom: The New Brain Science of Money, Happiness, and Success*, Mark Robert Waldman and Chris Manning, PhD, discuss how to balance your brain between the messy and organized network. Here is how it works: focus, relax, daydream, and then mindfully observe. The unconscious part of our brain is messy, and that's good, because our brain needs this to solve potential problems in a highly creative way. But there is another part of your brain, your conscious mind, that needs to be highly organized.

The imagination center and the thinking center, as they are called, alternate our thinking back and forth between being focused and creative imagination. When one turns on, the other turns off. If this process becomes unbalanced, many different emotions and psychological problems can show up in your life. The authors go on to say, "Anxiety can show up if you spend too much time in imagination, and if you spend too much time being highly focused, you will experience burnout, and your ability to be sensitive to other people's feelings and needs will deteriorate." I personally know all about this, being a real estate agent with deadlines.

The authors continue, "It's very important that you learn to relax your busy mind and allow yourself to daydream several times a day. If you become conscious and use mindfulness with your thinking and imagination, they can work together to help find solutions to problems. Then your intuition can be found with this practice."

These authors are world-renowned for their neuroscientific research on spirituality and consciousness. They say that "your intuition is found through a process that takes place in the salience network of your brain." It is stimulated by contemplative meditation and positive prayer. Their brain research shows that if you can enter into a state of relaxed mindful awareness, it is the only known strategy that allows you to observe how your mind and imagination are either working together or against each other.

For more balance between your mind and your imagination, they say to try this experiment:

> As you've been reading this, your mind should have been highly focused; now close your eyes and do 3 mindful yawns, notice how each yawn subtly changes your mental state or mood. Then spend 60 seconds doing super slow micro-movements, (so tiny it barely looks like you are moving) with your head and/or torso. ... If you go slowly enough, you will feel all kinds of tiny aches, and if you pause and yawn, that pain will often disappear. Once you are fully relaxed and alert in the present moment, you can watch how dozens of potential thoughts and feelings are floating around in your subconscious imagination center. You can observe painful memories and worries without being overwhelmed or anxious by your emotions."

Here's the best thing they have discovered: Stay mindfully relaxed and aware, then ask your inner being for new and creative solutions to any problem. Just take the time to listen to that inner wisdom, and you may hear an important clue or insight. Then meditate and affirm that intuition for a few moments before throwing yourself back into work and focus. They say to repeat this once or twice an hour throughout your day, and you will have created the perfect balance between the thinking and imagination centers of your brain (along with other networks). As they write, "This process is the best formula for happiness and success that neuroscience has to offer. It increases empathy, compassion, forgiveness and self-love."

Learning about this and other neuroscience research has helped me personally to recover from my own workaholic tendencies. My life was all about work and how I could make myself feel like I was enough. I learned and kept learning from all the books, workshops, and retreats over the last twenty-seven years that my mind was working more often than relaxing my mind through meditation and affirmations. I became very burned out in the fashion industry, and my emotions and anxiety lead to my sickness with ulcers.

Worry was the emotion that caused me to hit rock bottom in my career—worry that I was not good enough. Through contemplation and therapy, I discovered my worry of not being a good mom for my kids and not being a good enough wife for my husband while trying to focus on my work and travel for my worth. The imbalance caused my emotions and anxiety to take over. I was at the lowest point in my life. I was not balanced in either work or life. I learned from workshops and studying that there was only one way to heal, and that was to change my thoughts.

Thought are things, and things can
be changed.—Louise Hay

If you change the way you look at things, the
things you look at will change.—Wayne Dyer

Once I started practicing being more aware of my thoughts, slowing down and meditating, and using yoga for learning to breathe—yes, I just said that, *learning to breathe*—I found that the creative side of my brain could balance with my inner being. I started to focus on my health. I discovered every day that I was enough and I could have it all if I opened my mind to this *feeling of having enough and* with gratitude for what I had already. My inner being knowing that I was enough was a thought I brought into my consciousness by affirming, "I am enough! I have enough to share," and by asking myself how I could find my purpose in this life without stress. It led me to where I am today, writing a book about how to align yourself with the universe to manifest the life of your dreams.

Using the things, I have learned to help others has become my balance between work and life. I have found my purpose, my joy, and my compassion for others. I have found my true success by discovering my authentic self—the self that is enough, the thoughts that I am enough, and loving who I am every day through balancing my brain. By loving myself and believing in abundance vs. scarcity, I have attracted all of the things and thoughts that I needed to heal my life, heal my soul, and in turn heal my body. I have faith that you can also find your inner being in balance by reading this book.

When you go out into the woods, and you look at trees, you see all these different trees. And some of them are bent, and some of them are straight, and some of them are evergreens, and some of them are whatever. And you look at the tree and you allow it. You see why it is the way it is. You sort of understand that it didn't get enough light, and so it turned that way. And you don't get all emotional about it. You just allow it. You appreciate the tree. The minute you get near humans, you lose all that. And you are constantly saying, "You are too this, or I'm too this." That judgment mind comes in. And so I practice turning people into trees. Which means appreciating them just the way they are.—Ram Dass

Try doing this exercise daily: When you awake in the morning, instead of jumping out of bed and heading to the bathroom, sit up in bed and allow your senses to explore. Allow yourself to think of one or two things you are grateful for. Breathe a deep breath and stretch your hands to the ceiling. Allow the blood from your sleepy head to go through your outstretched hands down your arms into your shoulders and then down to your waist, then get out of bed with purpose. Don't pick up your cell phone or read any emails or watch any news; just allow yourself to be open to the day as it progresses for you. If you can just give yourself one hour to read positive books or write in a journal or exercise, then you have allowed yourself to go with the flow, and you are on your own agenda, not anyone else's—at least for the first hour in your day.

CHAPTER 3

Learning

*The best way to find yourself, is to lose yourself
in the service of others. Mahatma Gandhi.*

Our lives are spent learning—learning from failure and learning from accomplishments. Scientists have studied the brain and found that human children learn more in their first seven years than for the rest of their life. So think about all the things you may have learned from your parents, from your friends, from your teachers, coaches, etc.

We are constantly learning. Some of our beliefs about things come from experience, and those beliefs around the experience could be wrong. As we learn at a young age, our minds are like sponges, absorbing all that is new and exciting. These can be positive experiences, but we also can learn from bad experiences, and the beliefs that follow from them can stay with us for a short time, a long time, or our entire life. We sometimes learn desires from things that bring us pleasure, and we also learn from things we don't like, such as negative experiences.

Remember: you are the meaning of all the things you have learned from the past and are learning in the present, and you become what you desire or what you don't want. Learning how to let go of past programming is one of the things you can do to live a life of less resistance. We talked about this in the chapter on *allowing*. When you are learning to let go of resistance, you are learning not to react so quickly.

For example, if something doesn't go as planned, and you learned as a young child that if you yelled and screamed for something, your parents would be quick to react and give you want you desired so that you would be happy and quiet, think how that might not be the best way to react as an adult. If you scream and cry for what you want and throw a fit, other adults might call you childish or a brat. We must learn that some of our behaviors need to be changed so that we can attract the best for ourselves through the path of least resistance.

As you are opening up and allowing more into your life, instead of blocking, you will start to learn more techniques for letting go. If you learn to love yourself for who you are now instead of who you were in the past, or things that may have happened to you in the past, you start to learn to just be you. And being you is the best and most authentic thing you can do, for the most happiness.

Learning something new every day will help your mind, your soul, and your whole body. As we learn, our brains are actually creating new cells, and the more knowledge we have of something, over time, the more we create mastery. Every day, something new is being created. Scientists are still learning about the brain, and as humans, we are constantly evolving. You can learn so many new ways of doing things that can save more time and make your life or the life of someone you love better.

We live in a day and age where all we have to do to learn something new is go to YouTube, ask our phones, or have artificial intelligence think for us. The younger generation these days can get answers to problems in seconds, where in the past, it could take days, months, and sometimes years to try something with experiments and learn the outcome.

Scientists and doctors are learning more and more each day about neuroscience and the brain's neuroplasticity. They are discovering that the brain actually changes when we think positive and also changes when we think negative. They are also learning that if we change our thoughts on what we see, the thing we see will also change.

This is fantastic! All of this new science explains why positive psychology can help heal. Feeding your brain with good thoughts, gratitude, and positive affirmations can help with this brain neuroplasticity to give us more confidence and more joy, which leads to more creativity.

Try this exercise and see what you learn from it: Write down as many things as you can about where you feel you may have failed in life. Now, next to the things you feel you have failed at, write down what you learned from the experience. What I personally learned from doing this exercise is that failing at something doesn't have to be negative. I believe that if I had not failed, I would not have learned. If I had not failed, I would not have lived to become the person I am today. From each failure, we learn two equally valuable lessons: that there was at least one reason we failed and that we can rebound from that failure.

Whenever you feel like you have failed and you need something to change your feelings about it, look in a mirror and say to yourself the following affirmation from Louise Hay:

> I truly believe that my highest good is unfolding. When I am faced with a challenge or obstacle in life (which is bound to happen because it is just life), I am comforted with the power of my beliefs. The Universe has got my back, and I can trust that the spirit within me knows that nothing is impossible. All I need to move forward is to release any fear or judgment with the situation and just believe. With belief that all is well, my body, mind, and soul are always seeking expression. I can release any expectations and just believe that, however events manifest, my highest good is always unfolding. I can feel trust and relaxation as I let go of fear and truly trust the Universe. I allow myself to be guided in the direction of the highest and best outcome. Learning to allow this helps to put me on the path of least resistance. I can release any concerns about challenging events and their outcomes. All I need to do is believe and then turn it over to the Universe with total trust that all is well.

In Louise Hay's workbook *Love Yourself: Heal Your Life*, she discusses seven power points. Post these points somewhere so that you can memorize them and make them concepts as part of your belief system. You will soon see a different perspective in your life and begin attracting positive beliefs that the universe will bring better results to you.

Here are the power points:

1. We are each responsible for our own experiences.
2. Every thought we think is creating our future.
3. Everyone is dealing with the same damaging patterns of resentment, criticism, guilt, and hatred.
4. These are only thoughts, and thoughts can be changed.
5. We need to release the past and forgive everyone.
6. Self-approval and self-acceptance, in the now, are the keys to positive change.
7. The point of power is always in the present moment.

The object is to read these and not get stuck in a specific problem. You have the power to change. The object is to change what you believe about yourself and the world you live in.

Learn to understand yourself more—your inner self, your spiritual self—and operate under the power that was created only by you. Another affirmation we can use is, "I give myself permission to learn." We will talk more about affirmations in the next chapter.

I learned so much from listening to a podcast called "Learning How to Learn" by Jim Kwik. Our minds are more expansive than many people believe. Learn to develop a super-memory. Jim's work is shaking up the world's ways of teaching and learning, expanding the brain's capacity to learn. *Metalearning* is what he calls it. Here are the words to remember: *learn, retain, remember, repeat.*

Knowledge is power, and knowledge is profit. Your brain is your most powerful and profitable asset. We are taught to underestimate our learning capacity and that learning is fixed. Jim teaches how to use your "super brain." He is helping people to learn how to learn. He thinks we are drowning in information overload and our brains can easily shut down.

When I teach my courses to other real estate agents, I use Jim's memory technique on how to remember everyone's name. My seminars turn out better because this helps people feel important during my workshops.

We always seem to have excuses. "If you argue with your limitations, you get to keep them," says Jim. There are currently no schools that teach you how to learn. Learning is remembering, and retaining what you learn is a skill. How much time can you save? Learning is not a fixed capacity. Your mind never shuts off.

Jim Kwik suggests the following morning routine for creating and learning new habits:

1. Remember your dreams.
2. Make your bed.
3. Brush your teeth with the opposite hand.
4. Drink eight ounces of water—we are 70 percent water.
5. Take a cold shower. This resets the nervous system and helps with inflammation.
6. Drink "brain tea"—ginkgo biloba—to increase energy
7. Keep a journal.
8. Don't look at your phone for the first hour. It trains you to be reactive. You give away your sovereignty.
9. List three things you can do to win the day.
10. Have a brain smoothie: blueberries, avocado, broccoli, coconut oil.
11. Focus on reading—try to read one book a week. First you create habits, then habits create you.
12. Meditate/practice mindfulness—alpha wave states, visualizations.
13. Exercise. Five minutes of exercise in the morning starts your body for the best day.

There is one grand lie that we are limited. The only
limits we have are the limits we believe.—Wayne Dyer

In Jim Kwik's book *Limitless*, he discusses the seven lies of learning. He asks the reader this question: What are the most limiting myths you tell yourself? He calls lies "limited ideas entertained." You can ask yourself, *How can I turn these lies or limiting beliefs into positive ones?* By examining Jim Kwik's "Seven Lies of Learning," I believe you can replace them with positive beliefs and become a better learner, which is the third step to the word *balance.*

Here are the seven lies that Jim Kwik mentions in his book *Limitless*:

1. **Intelligence is fixed.** This belief is a very subtle one that we may not consciously think about, but it is programmed into our minds, usually from a young age. There is a belief that it is impossible to improve your life or change things because that is just the way things are. If that is the belief that is guiding your mindset, it is very hard to accomplish change or improvement.

   Carol Dweck, in her book *Mindset*, describes the difference between a fixed and a growth mindset. In a fixed mindset, students believe their abilities, their intelligence, and their challenges are just fixed traits. In a growth mindset, students understand that their challenges and abilities can be developed through effort, good teaching, and persistence.

   For example, consider Sir Richard Branson, owner of Virgin Industries. If he had a fix mindset, he would say, "I have dyslexia; I will never learn." With a growth mindset, he can say, "I have dyslexia, and I can learn by trying harder and practice."

2. **We only use 10 percent of our brains.** Kwik discusses that this myth has been around for many years, and there is no one direct source of where it comes from, but many have heard it from TV, maybe a movie, or many books over the centuries that man has been studying the brain. He lists several studies and overwhelming evidence to back up the truth that we use 100 percent of our brains. The key is to learn how.

3. **Mistakes are failures.** Kwik presents Einstein as a perfect example of someone who made lots of mistakes that were considered to be failures but were really just new ideas inspired by experimenting. Einstein is famously quoted as saying that a person who never makes mistakes never tried anything new. Kwik points out that you are not your mistakes; mistakes don't make you, they are just stepping-stones to rise to the next level. It is how we deal with them that defines us. There is no such thing as failure, only failure to learn.

4. **Knowledge is power.** Kwik agrees that knowledge is important, but it does not have any power unless there is an action being

performed with it. It is how you use your knowledge that is powerful. Kwik's belief is that knowledge times action equal power.

5. **Learning new things is difficult.** Learning won't always be super-easy, but by taking small steps and being consistent and persistent, anyone can learn something new and thrive at it. Break it down and understand that learning is a subset of methods—a process that can be fun, easy, and enjoyable.

6. **Criticism of other people matters.** This one is huge for me and all ties back to the programming in my mind that I am not good enough. Kwik explains that people will doubt you and criticize you no matter what you do. You will never know your true potential until you break the unfair judgments that you place on yourself. Don't allow other people's opinions and expectations to run or ruin your life, and I can add this: "What you think about me is none of my business."

7. **Genius is born.** Kwik tells a wonderful story of Bruce Lee and how it was through years of learning from other masters of kung fu and its philosophy that he became a master teacher and a philosopher himself. Kwik says the truth behind this myth that a genius is born is that there is always a method, not magic, and it is accomplished through deep practice.

Let's talk now about earth school versus society school. Earth school can provide us with a lifelong journey of learning. Earth school provides us with an education of the heart and of the soul. Societal school is learned with the mind; from birth to death, we learn from experiences of our own and also learn from the experiences of others. We can evolve and expand our thinking from life lessons learned in earth school. Life lessons can take on many forms, and we can face lots of challenges through these different forms of learning.

The majority of our learning is from experience. Some experiences are wonderful and provide a feeling of and a lesson in love. But if we learn from experiences, we all know that some of the experiences we go through will be chaotic and so challenging at times that we never want that experience again. What if we learned without judging the situation or circumstance and just trusted more in the universe and the earth school concept?

We are free to choose and close our minds from earth school, or we can choose to view the built-in lesson learned by being aligned with the universe. We can choose to consciously be aware of important lessons when they are right in our face, and we can gradually, objectively look at what we can learn from the experience (bad or good).

Learning to Listen

When I teach my classes to real estate brokers, I help them to understand the power of their words as well as the power to listen—and listen with true compassion. The three words that are most powerful are "Tell me more." Learning to listen after you say those three words is healing.

> *Deep listening is the kind of listening that can*
> *help relieve the suffering of another person. ... You*
> *listen with only one purpose: to help them empty*
> *their heart.—Thich Nhat Hanh*

When you say the words, "Tell me more," you are offering the sacred gift of listening instead of correcting someone's feelings. Corrective listeners are those who listen but then offer new ways to correct your feelings. Sometimes the corrective listener can make others feel like they are weak if they can't make those changes at that time in their life. The "tell me more" listener is in no rush to fix someone's sadness, fear, or anger. This type of listening is showing that you are simply there to be with others through the most painful situations. Your intention is to allow them to empty their heart, which is truly healing.

Joseph Campbell has a classic story called "Hero's Journey." There is a necessary point in travelers' evolution when they enter an abyss or the deconstruction of what was in order to be reborn into a new paradigm of being. Based on this story, the "tell me more" listener becomes the ally who walks with, not for, the emerging hero in a pivotal moment of learning. Travelers can awaken to their own innate illumination rather than become dependent on another bondage. They learn the truth.

We are constantly learning from the decisions that we make. If your inner being is in balance, you will discover that making decisions is easier and you can trust more in yourself.

In any moment of decision, the best thing you can do is the right thing, the next best thing is the wrong thing, and the worst thing you can do is nothing.—Theodore Roosevelt

President Roosevelt was considered a president who lived outside of the box of traditional leader thinking. He was what you would call a maverick. He lived with the knowledge that life is about creating and that life also includes making mistakes. He often talked about how important it was to make decisions in life, whether they were the right decision or not.

We can get frozen with fear, and fear is not forward thinking. We will always be faced with making decisions, and some will be very painful, but the only way to grow and learn is to take charge of our own lives. We will grow from trying our best and learning to make the best decision possible.

Making powerful decisions will propel us into the quantum leap of moving forward, but staying in the now is just as important. Do not put your goals into the future; just know that the decision to focus on your goals is in the present moment and visualizing those goals as true in the present moment will help manifest them. Your future is in the present moment. If a course of action is in alignment with what the universe wants, it will become empowered by your decisions and conscious manifestation.

Ask yourself these questions before reading any further, and hold the answers in your heart:

1. What does the universe want to manifest through you?
2. What is your true purpose on this earth?
3. How can you manifest balance between your work and your life?
4. Who are the people who should be joining you in reading this book?
5. Can you say aloud, "I have the freedom to dream big and the power of manifestation to make my dreams come true"?

Learning from Change

The only constant in life is change. Since every molecule in your body is changing every second and every day, you must accept this without judgment and without stress as much as possible. I personally love change. My career in real estate is the perfect choice for me, as each client and each transaction is different. No transaction will be the same, even if I sell the same house multiple times.

My brain and my body must be prepared for this type of job, because I am dealing with people and their dreams, and also, it involves people's money. I want to influence my clients positively with my positive energy. That way, I attract to me people who will respect my knowledge and expertise as I respect them for their desires and listen to what they want, not what I want for them. I learn from them how they want to be treated.

One person's personality is never the same as someone else's. Maybe some people have some of the same personality traits, but no one is ever the same as another person. I really enjoy this part of my job, and it shows. People like learning about me too.

When it comes to changing and adapting after we have learned that maybe we need to be open to change, just remember that we are all capable of change. If love and caring is the main ingredient for change, then change will become easier. Here is a list of questions you can review and then think about changing and adapting to something new. You can learn more about yourself by asking these questions:

- What in life is my greatest challenge? How can I love it and change my thoughts about it?
- Why can't I find the partner I am seeking? How do I let go and just love myself so I can change the energy of always feeling needy or that I need someone?
- Why do I overeat and not exercise? How can I love my body more and change my habits to become healthier?
- Why am I so miserable at my job? How can I change my thoughts about my work, and how I can serve others instead?

All of these questions are ways to change how you feel or look at the questions and then just look at them with love. When there is love, there is no fear of changing. Fear and love cannot exist in the same feeling at the same time. So when you replace fear with love, you are actually not thinking so much about yourself anymore, just thinking about the situation objectively so you can see positive change.

Changing can also bring about things that cause chaos, because when you open yourself up to change and learning to act and feel differently, your ego will come alive and be there to constantly remind you how hard it is to change, how stupid it is to think differently, and how much easier it will be to stay the same and not grow and learn. But in life, we must grow, and the more we grow, the more we change into the happy person we desire to be.

When you have the energy of a happy person, it is easier to attract the things you desire, because your vibrations will change to a frequency of the same things that are already seeking you. You will learn to become a magnet of the abundance and prosperity you desire, because love is the principle behind it, not fear. So start learning to change your feelings about something you aren't happy about, and it will change your vibrations. Change is good.

Learning with Regard to Money and Success

Have you ever noticed that there are not a lot of things taught in grammar school, middle school, high school, and even college about building wealth? Have you heard of money consciousness? I teach a workshop on that topic, and the methods I teach are very different from what you may have learned about money and how to attract more of it.

I have been an entrepreneur for over twenty five years now. I decided at an early age that I was tired of the corporate world making my employer a billionaire, when I wanted to create a business that I could run myself and manifest myself into a millionaire/billionaire. It took books like *Think and Grow Rich* by Napoleon Hill, *You Were Born Rich* by Bob Proctor, and *Rich Dad, Poor Dad* by Robert Kiyosaki for me and my husband to learn how to become rich. The book *Ninja Selling* by Larry Kendall helped me expand my real estate business, and it was the book *The Answer: Grow Any*

Business, Achieve Financial Freedom, and Live an Extraordinary Life by John Assaraf, that helped me explode my real estate business by changing my mindset about money.

What I learned from all of these books is that money is energy, and we must have positive money consciousness and awareness before we can attract more money to us. Our inner being can be in perfect alignment with the energy of money when we are open to receiving it, instead of putting up resistance to the flow of money into our lives with negative subconscious thoughts about money. Because I learned how to be open to receiving abundance, and I have learned that what you think about comes about and what you focus on expands, I would like to share with you some of the miracle that happened to me once I changed my money mindset.

Once I began to learn more about real estate—investing in it and helping others invest in it—my whole life changed for a wealthier future. All of the authors of the above-mentioned books also believe that owning and investing in real estate is the foundation to becoming independently wealthy and the first step to having financial freedom.

My first real estate purchase came at the age of twenty-three. My firstborn son made his at age twenty-one, because I passed down the knowledge of how you can earn passive income through real estate. I have helped hundreds of people buy and sell real estate. The more I help and serve people with a real estate transaction, the more I attract others who have been referred to me to help them with their goals of buying and selling real estate. I am known as HUD Queen, Mountain Monica (for helping people invest in real estate at Colorado resorts), and a 100 percent full-on ninja in the real estate sales training of hundreds of real estate brokers.

It starts with your mindset. Once my husband and I learned more about how to buy distressed properties, fix them up, and resell them, I had more people wanting to learn this wealth-building technique too. On our first deal, we earned $78,000, then another at $60,000, and another at $80,000. Over the past four years—using a method called a 1031 exchange that we learned from other investors and our CPA is a legal way to buy and sell real estate without having to pay income taxes on the money you earned from the sale of an investment property—we generated over $350,000 by fixing and flipping resort properties in Winter Park, Colorado. We rolled all that money into the purchase of our dream home in Grand Lake, a resort in Colorado surrounded by three large lakes and a small community where we would like to retire.

Could all this have happened by circumstance and no planning? I doubt it. We had to have a plan and ask others for help. We had to have confidence and the will to learn. We also had to have a burning desire to manifest the dream home into our lives and a positive money consciousness.

Real estate is an asset that is tangible and increases in value over time. The year 2020 has been a year of unknowns in businesses and livelihoods. The virus called COVID-19 has been the biggest unknown in our entire world. But, because I believe that my family and I deserve the best lives, our real estate business has not been hurt. In fact, we have been considered an essential business throughout the pandemic shutdown. By using our intuition, webinars, and online conferences, 2020 has been the best year of my twenty-seven-year career in real estate. Our properties have increased in equity, and if you add it all up, since our first home purchase in 1990, we have earned well over a million dollars. That comes out to $33,333 per year of increased wealth on top of our daily job, as real estate broker. Adding up the income my husband, my son, and I have created over the last eight years, the total is over $3 million, and we are all living debt-free.

How did this happen? Once I decided that I wanted to be a millionaire, I had to deliberately visualize myself as such. I visualized what it looked like to have $100,000 in savings. I visualized living without any debt. Most of all, I changed my beliefs of knowing that I could have whatever my mind believed I could have. I changed my mindset about money, and I started to attract the right people to help me achieve my goals of financial freedom. It really doesn't matter what type of business you want to manifest as long as it makes sense, is a passion, and you are willing to learn.

The problems that most people have are their past conditioning around the topic of money. Thoughts are still in our subconscious from years of programming as a child around money. Let's do this simple exercise: write down some things you heard your parents, grandparents, or even teachers say when it came to money, or simply describe an experience you may have had as a child with regard to something you wanted and were told by and adult that you couldn't have it or your family couldn't afford it.

Here are some of the sayings that I heard:

- Money doesn't grow on trees.
- Rich people are snobs.
- You have to work really hard to be rich.
- More money, more problems.
- Money is dirty.

An experience I remember very clearly is having nice things for a little while and then not having nice things. It was all ups and downs and a lot of stress around money, especially when my parents got divorced. I remember my parents yelling about money. I remember being told we couldn't afford some things I wanted and that my father was to blame for not sending child support or alimony. I am not blaming my parents for the unfortunate way I learned about money and its scarcity. I just know that as I grew up, a lot of the things I learned from them became rooted in my subconscious.

As an adult, I continued to think of money as scarce. I would go through the same cycle of having money, then not having money, and experiencing the roller coaster of stress each month. Once I learned that I could reprogram and change by beliefs about money, everything in my life changed too.

Here is what needs to happen for you to reprogram your money consciousness. We talked in earlier chapters about believing and allowing, which will help you to learn about reprogramming with your belief that you deserve all the abundance that is available to you from source energy or the universe, as I call it. You must open your mind to changing these negative subconscious thoughts about money and allow money and abundance to flow easily to you with less resistance.

Here is a simple way to work on your mindset about money and start to attract the right people to help you achieve not only your financial goals but your personal life goals too. Ask yourself, "What is more valuable than money?" Here are some possible answers:

- family
- health
- freedom
- peace
- serving others

- passions
- success

Now, after reviewing this list, ask yourself, "Would more money in my life help with all these things that are more valuable than money?"

Next, think about your biggest problems or current concerns. They may include the following:

- feeling stuck in a job you hate
- low self-esteem or self-worth
- lack of confidence
- lack of money
- believing it's too hard to change things now
- procrastinating with achieving your goals
- fear of failure

How can you learn to look at these problems differently and change your thoughts about them?

First, in order to achieve a new mindset about money, life, and financial goals, you must do the following five things:

1. Retrain your brain.
2. Develop new beliefs.
3. Get clear and confident.
4. Master your emotions.
5. Know that you deserve the best and will not settle for less.

These five simple things are easy to do but also easy not to do. It will all be based on learning and your level of commitment—not just being interested in changing but truly committed to take the steps needed to reprogram your subconscious. I have seen some of my students go from having no self-worth to reprogramming their brain with creative visualizations, financial success meditations, affirmations, and changing beliefs to becoming rich beyond their wildest dreams.

What I learned from John Assaraf and his neural reconditioning process is that we only need about thirty minutes a day for about ninety days to reprogram our financial consciousness. There will be more effort in the first thirty days using your conscious mind with regard to your desires, your will power, and your persistence. Then things start to change with practice and become more subconscious, where you will behave automatically by the rewiring of your brain.

Reprogramming your brain is like planting a seed that will grow, expand, and then reproduce again. You soon realize that you are limitless. We will talk more about how to expand your mind in a later chapter. Just know that you can learn with a little intensity in the beginning, but the more and more you learn, the more the intensity gains around your thoughts about money and abundance. So essentially, your alignment with the source energy of money will grow. You just have to open your mind to learning and be committed. Then miracles will happen!

CHAPTER 4

Affirming

*People do not seem to realize that their
opinion of the world, is also a confession of
character. Ralph Waldo P Emerson.*

hat are affirmations? For those of you who are a little familiar
with the benefits of positive affirmations, I would like to
explain them a bit more. An affirmation is really anything
that you say or think. A lot of what we say and think is quite negative
and does not create good experiences for us at all. We have to retrain our
thinking and speaking into more positive patterns if we want to change
our lives for the better. If we want to find more balance, we actually have
to have more positive affirmations.

This is the beginning point of your path to change. In essence, you are
trying to say things with your subconscious mind. What comes up for you
when you fail at something? What are the affirmations that come up? Do
you think, *I am so stupid. I am so disorganized. I cannot believe I just did
that. I hate myself for doing that.* These are all negative affirmations. What
if you had an affirmation that said *I am taking responsibility. I am aware
that there is something that I can do to change.*

This is a way for us to start talking about affirmations and then doing
these affirmations. We want to eliminate a lot of things in our lives that
somehow bring up negativity. Every thought you think and every word

you speak is an affirmation. A lot of our self-talk and our internal dialogue is just a stream of affirmations. You are using affirmations every single moment, whether you know it or not. You are affirming and creating all your life experiences with every word and every thought.

So guess what? If thoughts are things, then we can change these things. Your beliefs are merely habitual thinking patterns that you learned as a child. We talked about this in the chapter on believing. Many of them work very well for you, but there is another belief that may be limiting you.

We are programmed from the day we are born until the day we die. Our programming is always there, in the back of our mind. It is in our subconscious. It is made up of things we learned from our parents, from our teachers, from our peers. Every time you get angry with someone, you are affirming that you want more anger in your life. Every time something bad happens to you and you feel like you are victim, you are actually affirming that you want to continue to feel like a victim. If you feel that life is not giving you what you want, then of course you won't get what you want until you change the way you think and talk.

You are not a bad person for thinking the way you do. We have all had parents who probably did not know they were saying things that were negative to us, that they were programming us. They thought they were teaching us about life the way their parents taught them. It is time to wake up and stop consciously creating the life we do not want and start creating the life we do want. You can do this. I have done it. We can all do it. We just need to learn how.

Okay, so how do affirmations work? An affirmation in itself is just a statement. It can be positive or negative. So, when you say, *Oh! This is stupid* or *I know it will not work*, which affirmation do you think will turn out? Of course, the negative one. But if you say *My prosperity is growing* and *I am open to abundance*, guess what happens? You will be open to these positive affirmations. Every day you affirm, more of that will become true in your life. You will be aligning yourself with the universe. The universe will hear these affirmations, and they will win.

A lot of people complain. Complaining is a negative affirmation. If you think about the times you have complained about something, what turned out from that? Try putting a rubber band around your wrist, and every time you are about to complain about something, pop that rubber band on your wrist. That feeling of instant pain will cause you to not want to complain.

Affirmations are like seeds. They are planted in soil. If you have poor soil, you will have poor growth. That's what complaining does. It does not help you to grow. Rich soil and abundant growth will happen with positive affirmations.

The more you choose to think thoughts that make you feel good, the more quickly these affirmations will work. Happy thoughts are very simple and very doable. The way you choose to think right now is a choice. You may not realize it because you thought this way for so long, but it really is a choice, and you can always choose again.

I have been using affirmations for many years. I was using affirmations for my health before I started using them in my business. I was using them in my personal and spiritual life, and there were a lot of books I would read on affirmations. I think those from Louise Hay were probably the best on affirmations and how the law of attraction works. I know affirmations might not work 20 percent of the time, but what if they worked 80 percent of the time?

There was a yoga teacher, Maureen McGuinness, who said to repeat this every day: "Yesterday is history, tomorrow is a mystery, today is a gift, which is why we call it the present." What a wonderful affirmation to repeat!

You can choose to feel good in this moment, and you can create your future from these moments. Once you have done your affirmation, it is time to just release and let it go into the universe. The universe has your back. You can make affirmations in both thought and word. Release them to the universe so that the law of attraction can bring them to you.

How does this work? The universe is far more clever than we are, and it does not judge or criticize. It just goes with what your thoughts are and your affirmations. It is not your job to figure out how to bring your affirmations to fruition. You just need to use them and let them go.

Let's say you are declaring *My income is increasing and all abundance is coming to me easily and effortlessly.* I use that affirmation a lot with my business and with my coaching, but what if you have this old programmed belief that you do not deserve to have your income increase? What if your subconscious belief about money is that money is not good? My belief system, when I was growing up, was that money was scarce. I heard my mother say a lot, "We cannot afford that." As little children, we start to believe these things about life, and we continue to operate under those assumptions for the rest of our lives—until we choose to really look at these affirmations we have been saying over and over in our head.

If prosperity is something you want more of, and you want more money in your life, then you need to come to terms with these negative perceptions. They have been affirmations for you and your family all these years, and it will be your job to turn those negative beliefs into positive affirmations. So let's start with some of these affirmations about money and abundance.

Since we are all born as creative beings, we can create what we want. We need to dream big! Let's try this experiment: Five years from now, what will your life look like? Write down everything that seems ideal and positive that you truly want. As an example, here are the five things I truly wanted when I did this exercise back in 2007:

- I want a successful marriage and a good relationship with my kids.
- I want a second home in the mountains near a resort.
- I want to have $100,000 in the bank.
- I want to help lots of people and be rewarded for my help.
- I want to relax and travel as much as I work. I want balance.

Okay, now you can look at your wants and create affirmations around them. Mine looked like this:

- I have total financial freedom in an easy and relaxed manner, in a good and essential way.
- Money flows easily and effortlessly to me.
- It feels great to have $100,000 or more in the bank.
- I love the mountain views from my condo in the mountains.
- I enjoy the company of my family.
- I enjoy closing forty or more real estate transactions per year.
- I am helping lots of people enjoy buying a home.

I truly believed in my affirmations and the power they have each time I say them, and here are the results:

- I have been successfully and happily married for thirty-four years. My relationship with my boys is everything I dreamed it could be.
- We bought three condos in the mountains of Winter Park ski resort and then sold them all to buy a large house in Grand Lake.
- I saved 20 percent of my money each time I was paid, and now have $100,000 and more in the bank.
- I close forty or more real estate transactions per year and have helped hundreds of people own a home.
- I relax in life with traveling to different places for vacation.
- I work fewer hours but get paid more.

People look at my life sometimes and say that I am lucky. But I know that we create our own luck. Luck is preparedness. It is where opportunity meets plans. I make a plan, and then I watch for the opportunity to achieve the plan. Plans will change, and then you will notice even more opportunity.

*Within every adversity, there is an equal
or greater benefit.—Napoleon Hill*

Try not to be overwhelmed by problems as you begin using affirmations in your daily life. What I have discovered is that when affirming what you want, be careful what you wish for. You are that powerful. Your affirmations will start changing a lot of things in your life. So I advise you to seriously look at where you want to be in five years and realize that your thoughts and affirmations will take on a life of their own.

You may have to give up something in order to receive that affirmation. You may have to lose a friend or a spouse or partner in order to achieve what you really want out of life. Just focus on the love instead of the doubts and fears in this type of situation. Know that love is the answer.

It is funny that in 2007, when I wrote down my five passions and where I saw myself in five years, I was very intuitive about the real estate market crash that was about to happen in 2008. Instead of allowing fear to consume me, I created affirmations for success. Instead of getting out of real estate, my focus turned to how I could help people when they were facing foreclosures. My job would be to serve people who were having a hardship. My plan was to become an expert in this field of real estate that was a huge unknown for the real estate community as well as everyone who owned a mortgage. It was a decision that was based on love and service to others. It was the pinnacle of the success that would follow into the future for the next twelve years.

There are lots of ways to use affirmations. Some can be around health, money, relationships, and work. Affirmations should always be used in the present moment, the present tense. They should be said with *I am* or *I have* or, to put a feeling to it, *I enjoy*. Putting your affirmations in the present tense will allow them to permeate into your consciousness. They will become more and more believable until eventually, they become who you are.

You must allow yourself to accept the goods whether you think you deserve them or not. This belief can come over as an affirmation that you practice and practice and practice until your universal mind sees that as your highest good. Combined with visualization, it can become a very powerful tool.

Just remember what Louise Hay says: "No matter how wonderful the present moment is, the future can be even more fulfilling, joyous." The universe is always waiting in smiling repose for us to align our thinking with its laws. When we are in alignment, everything will flow. It is all possible. You can do it. I can do it. We can all do it. Just make the effort, and you will be very pleased. Your whole world will change for the better, and you will be better with balance.

Affirmations for Health

- Every cell in my body is alive with health and energy.
- I sleep in peace and wake in joy.
- My body is strong and healthy.
- Every system in my body functions exactly as it was intended to.
- I easily choose to nurture my body with healthy foods.

- I am so grateful for my health and vitality.
- I pay attention and listen to what my body needs for health and vitality.
- I move and exercise my body in ways that feel good.
- My immune system is strong and healthy.
- I have excellent health practitioners who assist me in achieving and maintaining a strong, healthy body.
- I meditate daily to give my body deep rest and enhance my immune system.
- I am guided to any supplements to take for my health.
- I breathe deeply, bringing energy to all my cells.
- My body is flexible.
- My body has a remarkable capacity for healing.
- Every resource I need for my healing comes to me.
- I am so grateful for the beautiful way the trillions of cells in my body work together.

Pain is inevitable. Suffering is optional.—Buddha

Spiritual leader Ram Dass shared that we may elevate ourselves from being so identified with our pain by not referring to it as "my pain" but as "the pain." It is important to fully feel the feeling whenever it visits, but don't allow it to become you. It is also important to realize that "the pain" is not unique to you, and to know that others are also experiencing "the pain." You are never alone in your suffering, and you can allow the feeling to be released out into the universe. You can use the experience of release to help others. In other words, witness it, allow it, then release it. A Japanese poet, Kenji Miyazawa, said, "We must embrace 'the Pain' then burn it as fuel for the journey." Love allows our wounds to become wisdom. Then your wisdom can help others.

A wonderful example of this freedom from suffering that I personally experienced is with my diagnosis of hyperthyroid disease. I decided not to let the disease claim me or become me. I was able to shine love on my situation, be objective to it, not fear it, and allow the disease to be released from my consciousness. My journey of two years with this pain and suffering never became me, because I loved it and affirmed it to leave me.

My body was healed, and I gained wisdom from this healing. Now I can share this wisdom with you.

There are many people who believe that affirmations are just wishes, and most wishes don't come true. But what if you could help those wishes come true by putting the affirmations into action? Since thoughts are things, and things are real, our thoughts can transform our wishes into affirmations and our affirmations into action. From action, we get the promised results.

I teach how affirming works in my Ninja Selling classes. I have seen my students write this affirmation twenty-five times a day: "I enjoy earning [a specific dollar amount] or more per year." They write it for thirty days. What happens is a miracle. If they take action with the affirmation, they get results. They don't just wish it, they actively take action on how it feels to earn that specific dollar amount. By putting a feeling of the word *enjoy* into the daily affirmation, they are programming their mind to believe they can have this joy.

I have used this same affirmation to increase my income by 300 percent in a year's time. I manifested this miracle in my life so easily and effortlessly that I wanted to share it with everyone I met. I started teaching and coaching because I learned that affirmations work.

As I mentioned in an earlier chapter, when I was diagnosed with Graves' disease (strange that this is my last name), the endocrinologist told me he needed to remove my thyroid with a radioactive pill. I immediately said, "Hold on a minute! I am a teacher for Louise Hay's 'You Can Heal Your Life,' so I need to research this before I decide to remove an organ from my body!"

Don't get me wrong: I believe that doctors can heal people. But I wanted to try healing myself first. I am so glad that I listened to my inner voice. I knew I could heal, and I practiced affirmations for my thyroid every minute of the day for a little over a year, along with getting balanced with acupuncture and changing my diet. I would even sing an affirmation out loud while hiking with the dogs or taking a shower. It went like this: *I am at the center of life, and I love and approve of myself.* The more I loved myself and my thyroid, the better my dis-ease became.

The emotion that was tied to hyperthyroidism (Graves' disease) was a feeling that I wasn't getting to express my true self or was feeling left out.

The more my inner being was balanced with love affirmations, the more I was expressing my true self. I took the action needed after saying these affirmations along with being better balanced with food, exercise, and a weekly trip to the acupuncturist. I healed myself. I am proud to say that I am in full remission from this disease, and I have gone two years without any symptoms. You can research the list of emotions tied to diseases in Louise Hay's book *You Can Heal Your Life*.

Here are other Louise Hay affirmations that I use to start off my day each morning:

- My body is rested and my mind is clear. I start my day with positive thoughts.
- I am relaxed, nonresistant, and clear. My day unfolds with ease and grace. People support me throughout the day. The universe supports my desires today. I am open to receiving greatness.
- Creative possibilities are available to me. Nothing holds me back.
- I take action with faith and clarity.
- I am healthy, well, and vibrant. Today is a great day.
- I am having fun today.
- I bring joy to others.
- I bring light with me wherever I go.
- I am a positive influence on the world. All is well.

Try them, put feelings around them, and watch for miracles.

Establishing your own morning routine is essential to establishing good habits. This will help you to be better with balance. Starting your day with a morning routine is so important for your brain. The first thing I do when I wake up in the morning is lie there and think about what I want for the day. I also think about any dreams I might have had that can help me with how to plan my day.

The second thing I do is I say thanks. I give thanks to everything that is good for me. I give thanks for my family. I give thanks for the love that I have for my friends. I give thanks for food, shelter, and clothing. I lie there and just feel good about giving thanks.

The third thing I do is get out of bed and make my bed. I feel like making the bed is a very important part of my morning routine, because it starts me on the path to accomplishing tasks for the day. Also, when you come back from the day, you see that your bed is made.

The fourth thing I do is make coffee. While my coffee is brewing, I will do a few stretches and get my body into good form. Then, after I have my coffee, I sit down and read something positive. Reading something positive puts me in a good positive mindset. I also journal, so I take a few minutes to journal, and then after that I do my affirmations.

After affirmations, I feel really great, and that is when I will write two personal notes. These could be for work or they could be for family. They could be personal, and they could also help with being thankful. This my morning routine, and it helps me to establish good habits to start my day.

Another wonderful way to keep your inner being in balance is to create a nightly ritual. Just like a morning ritual, this is a way to end your day with a higher frequency that will connect and align you with the universe, as well as connecting you to the world with positive vibrations. If you can spend ten minutes on self-appreciation and counting your blessings as you lie in bed, you will find that your sleep will be more satisfying. You may experience dreams that you'll remember in the morning to use as guidance for the day ahead of you.

It's important not to watch the news or television shows that have negative visual scenes. Your subconscious will be taking a lot of those visuals into your brain, and that can sometimes cause negative dreams or nightmares. I have personally found that if I read something positive or just close my eyes while sitting up in bed and use visualization techniques to see how my future is becoming, I can then ask a question with the intention of getting answers while I sleep.

Using Imagination and Visualizations with Your Affirmations

Setting intentions, letting go of resistance, and expanding on what you desire by visualization that it has already happened can help you to realize that your dreams really can come true. When you are having issues with work or any relationship, the first thing to do is practice visualization while meditating on the problem. As you start to feel a sense of inner peace and harmony, you can begin to feel happier and more balanced, which can help you connect more meaningfully with your work or with a relationship that may have issues.

The problems in our relationships can often serve as a mirror of the disconnection we have with ourselves. If we can get closer to ourselves and clear with ourselves first, then we can improve our interactions with others. As we visualize ourselves with less tension and let go of negative thoughts about the situation, we will automatically feel lighter and happier. This feeling or vibrational frequency helps us to be more compassionate and loving, which in return will help the relationship to be more loving. When you address your own imbalance or your disharmony from within, you can start to develop the right mindset to improve all of your lived relationships.

Imagination stimulates the brain. From there, it stimulates progress and gives birth to change. Isn't the reason we are alive and living today is to give birth to change? To evolve and change for the better?

Think of a time when you were stuck in life. Maybe you feel stuck right now? Did you or do you want to move on with that feeling of doubt and worry, or did you or do you want to let go of the fear and just imagine that things can be better? Here is a great imagination exercise for when you feel stuck. It works best when you close your eyes.

Imagine yourself on a ship crossing the ocean to a new life and a new beginning. Life is like an ocean that has swells that toss up and down, but you can also see the ship moving calmly with the waves. When you are on top of a swell, you can see your future, and life feels positive and exciting, but you must also realize that your time at sea on this ocean ride can have its chaos of ups and downs. See and feel the calm. See and imagine the ship sailing smoothly through the water. Even with the ups and downs in the ocean waves, your ship is calm. Feel yourself bobbing up and down gently, and imagine each new wave as each new day. Feel the rhythm and breathe deeply into this rhythm. Now just imagine yourself becoming calm and enjoying the ride.

Affirmations are a powerful tool for aligning with the universe to manifest your desired reality. We consciously and subconsciously invite miracles into our lives when we practice saying, feeling, and imagining our affirmations. Just trust in the power of affirmations, and you will soon have your inner being in balance to very quickly make what you have stated as true become true.

CHAPTER 5

Nurturing

*Every day we are engaged in a miracle which we do
not even recognize: a blue sky, white clouds, green
leaves, the black curious eyes of a child and our own
two eyes. All is a miracle.—Thich Nhat Hanh.*

indfulness is a form of nurturing. Breathing is a form of
mindfulness. Ask yourself right in this very moment: how are
you breathing? Pause for a few seconds and be mindful of how
you are breathing and then read on. When you ask this question of how
you are breathing, ask also if it is deep or shallow, rapid or slow. Are you
holding your breath at any time, or is it a rhythmic cycle? Many people,
when asked this question about their breathing, tend to say they are not
even aware of their breathing or much less how they are breathing.

Another question while being mindful of your breath is, do you feel
blessed to breathe? So many people live their lives without being grateful
for breathing. Being aware of this amazing gift of breath opens a door to
living in the present moment. Breath is life itself. Breath is the first thing
we do out of the mother's womb and the last thing we do before we die.
Becoming aware of your miracle of breath is the first step to becoming
mindful of yourself, and it will help keep you in the present moment
instead of your thoughts being in the past of your yesterdays with blame

and guilt or too far into the future. Being more mindful of the present moment helps us not to project ourselves too far into the future.

Consciousness is manifested in the present moment. Aligning with the universe in the present moment will help you to find your inner balance. It will make peace with yourself and provide the nurturing that you need to feel safe and loved.

In the book *The Living Universe*, author Duane Elgin writes, "American Indian lore speaks of three miracles. The first miracle is that anything exists at all. The second miracle is that living things exist. The third miracle is that living things exist that *know* they exist. As human beings conscious of ourselves, we represent the third miracle." Self-awareness and the practice of mindfulness, nurturing, and loving ourselves would bring us into alignment with the universe and help us to be better with balance.

Let me ask you: how do you see the world? One of the major things I have changed with my thought is how I see the world. I now understand that how I see life is like a mirror reflecting back to me images of my own thinking. I now realize that by changing my thinking, I can change those reflections in the mirror. As we age, we bring years of beliefs, biases, and assumptions to the world that we look at. Who we are and who we have become is all from that programming that is all we have heard, experienced, and believed—mostly from our parents, but also from teachers, churches, friends, and family members.

We can fill our world with thoughts of fear, selfishness, and hatred, or we can live life as a joy, feel compassion, and have more love. Ask yourself: Do you see a world that can work for everyone? Do you surround yourself with people who are doing the best they can? Or do you see a world that is broken and you might as well give up?

Remember the mirror that I talked about earlier. What does it reflect back to you? Shakespeare said it best: "There is nothing good or bad, but thinking makes it so."

Why not reflect on joy, compassion and love? We can always choose love over hate, patience over irritation, and happiness over depression. Each time we choose, we are sending out new ripples or waves to the universe. When aligned with the universe, these actions will eventually return to us.

This is the law of cause and effect that we talked about earlier, and it is always at work, but it has no memory. The past is gone, so we always have a choice. We can release the mistakes, replace them with love, and the past will have no power over us. We can always choose again without judgment and without fear. We can start each new day in the present moment, and the past is always welcomed if we live with no regret. We can end the day with appreciation and love for ourselves and nurture our inner being, who is always loving back to us.

Nurturing with Zeal

When we talk about nurturing, what comes to mind? Do you think of a mother nurturing you? Do you think of a mother bird nurturing a baby bird by feeding it? In my mind, I think of how I treat myself and how I treat others. Do I nurture others with inspiration? How can I make someone's day?

I have been told by many people that I look like I have a lot of zeal in my life. I like the word *zeal*. When you think about it, zeal means to be happy, and I feel like when I use my gift of zeal, I am fully aligning myself with the universe and with my mind, my heart, and my body. Zeal will always propel me forward, because I am eager to share of myself.

Yet there is a balance between giving up myself and giving to others. Like an empty pitcher, I cannot fill others' cups until I have been replenished myself first. If you think about an airplane, when the flight attendant says you must put the oxygen over your face first before you help or assist another, that is really what we're talking about. You must nurture yourself first, practice regular self-care, and nurture all aspects of yourself before you can care for others.

When you are determined to care about someone else first, ask yourself, *What do I need to do first in order for me to help others?* I can effectively use zeal to better myself. Zeal is a gift that motivates us. It inspires others to seek out and find their spiritual truth. With zeal, we possess communication skills. We have empathy, intelligence, and other talents, but zeal is the gift that will actually help us better serve the world. Here is a great affirmation from nurturing: *I care for myself and others with passion and enthusiasm.* That is the kind of zeal I'm talking about.

I want you to spend some time on this exercise. List all the things you are passionate about and that add zeal to your life. From this list, look at how you can use this with others—how you can help others by showing them the passion and enthusiasm you have. I have been able to teach others by first looking at myself and what helps me.

We all have a unique way of seeing things, shaped by our experiences, our genetics, and the choices we make consciously to change our behavior or alter our moods. What's so cool is that we can change our behavior by changing the way we think, feel, and act. The believing part is important if you want to change your personality, and all it takes is practice. If you can actually release or surrender all of your beliefs for just a few minutes each day with meditation, and just open up to feeling love, your worries, fears, and doubts will disappear, and so will the personality that goes along with them.

We are all capable of having the life of our dreams. Aligning with the universe with love and joy and compassion for yourself shows a true capacity for nurturing. We have faith that all our old beliefs and limits will fade away as we accept the power of our limitless source. This source is love, and it nurtures us and guides us to being our bigger, better, more beautiful self.

When you let fear take the wheel, doubt, uncertainty, stress, and pain will be in the forefront of all your decisions. That is not a nurturing way to live. Your vibrations when you love yourself and are grateful for the others in your life attract a peaceful and loving vibration, which in turn nurtures your soul. As your soul is empowered with love, the life of your dreams becomes a reality.

Every day, you will be provided with new opportunities to improve yourself and develop new skills. You have a choice to love yourself more and express your unique talents or deny your true self and stay stuck in your old beliefs and habits. When you decide on believing in yourself, nurturing yourself, and living with faith, you will attract to you all your desires because of your loving vibrations. Work with the universe to attract and manifest your best life possible.

Aligning with the Universe

I have always believed that I am doing my best. Because of this belief, my energy has always been high and mostly positive. That is not to say that I have never experienced sadness or negative thoughts, but from a very early age, I have always believed that there is a higher source that I am connected to that only wants the best for me. I believe in angels; I believe that I can ask and I shall receive. But I have learned that in order to receive my highest and best life, I must feel and act as if it is already mine. Through this belief, many wonderful things have manifested for me, and I feel truly blessed for the life that I live.

What I have learned and am still learning is that I must be in alignment with this higher source—Universe, God, Spirit, or Nature. Whatever you want to call this connection, the practice of having your inner being in balance and connecting to this higher source is what I discovered is the reason for having this amazing life that I have cocreated.

I am writing this book because I feel and know with all my heart and soul that all humans can experience this bliss and joy in their lives. We all have the potential to be our biggest, brightest, and most beautiful self. We can shine our light so bright that it will permeate into the areas of darkness in this world and help to create a better place for all of us to live. I will take you through the steps that I believe will help you to align yourself with the universe. That will help you to balance with this higher source and manifest the life of your wildest dreams.

> *You can't always get what you want, but if*
> *you try sometimes, you just might find, you*
> *get what you need.—The Rolling Stones*

When you are playing the same vibrational harmony, the universe will pick up that vibration and match it with what you really need. It's not just what you are thinking but how you are feeling and believing that counts.

We must feel the presence of love, peace, joy abundance, health, and wholeness. We can do this by tuning our thoughts and beliefs in to positive vibrations. Then the universe will vibrate on that same note to produce our experience. So, if you aren't getting what you want, just try changing the frequency of your thoughts and emotions and you just might find, you get what you need.

My dreams came true as I put them into action. It is not enough for me to simply hope a dream will come true. I must take action. I can turn to my source of supply and allow the barriers to fall down around me, giving up the resistance of fear and doubt. I give my desires to my higher power and listen for answers and inspiration to come to me. I follow this divine guidance as I move closer in the direction of my dreams and allow them to become a reality.

It's said that we are born with only two fears: the fear of loud noises and the fear of falling. These are instinctual to human nature. All other fears are learned from experience. And we can grow or shrink from them.

There's a famous quote from Eleanor Roosevelt: "You gain strength, courage, and confidence by every experience in which you really stop to look fear in the face." Running away from your fear or around it can only stunt your growth. You must face it.

I always tell myself, "If I am not uncomfortable doing something new, then I am not growing." I might be afraid of asking for a raise or stopping a relationship that is not healthy, but when I face that fear, I can gain courage and see that the fear is imagined, not real. Then I move through it and live fearlessly.

Each time I experience growth instead of being static, I feel free and more in alignment with the universe. Ask for signs from your inner guidance as well as your spirit guides. My spirit guide has been Archangel Raphael. I discovered his presence many years ago as I was praying for a friend who had overdosed on drugs.

When we learn more about metaphysics, there are views within the practice that say the world is just an illusion and tend to see material things, such as our physical bodies, as not valuable. This has caused confusion that leads to disregarding the importance of taking care of ourselves physically. Some religions actually believe you only have to trust in God and you will be healthy; you don't need to use medicine or doctors when the body is sick. My view, and the view of my spiritual community, is that we must take action to heal and care for our bodies as one of the ways of self-expression and self-love. I choose to believe that our bodies are very wise and know what they need to last us a longer physical lifetime if we listen, learn, and nurture.

Science shows that if we get proper rest, nourishing food, the right exercise, and useful positive thoughts, our bodies benefit. The universe will support your right-thinking and positive nurturing of your body with excellent health and a longer time on this planet to help and serve others with your gifts. If you do fall ill, or an accident occurs that causes your body not to be in its most desired health, then allowing doctors and health practitioners who have studied your illness to guide you is important. You can help heal yourself along the way with positive affirmations and expressing love for your body and not judging it as a negative thing. Be grateful for the people and even the circumstances of your illness or disease, and the universe will give back to you the health you and your body, mind, and soul deserve.

Others who pray for you will benefit your desire to get well. We can't just wish for good health; it takes action on your part to nurture, care, and love your body enough to keep it from getting sick in the first place. Here is a wonderful affirmation from Dr. Margaret Stortz for loving and nurturing your body: "My body is one of my gifts, and I value its ability to be my current partner in life and to serve me well."

When we look at the value of our energy and apply it in our lives, it is very important to direct it positively. It is also important to be aware of your thoughts. Are you judging a situation negatively? If so, do you realize that you have a choice to see it differently? Are you wasting time and precious energy worrying and wondering what-if? Is there a way you can see the situation in a different light? Can you choose to be grateful instead of hateful?

Eleanor Roosevelt said, "It takes as much energy to wish as it does to plan." So if you can commit to taking your positive heart desires and creating a concrete positive action plan, you will be using energy in a positive way for pursuing all your desires.

Relax!

Relaxation is a big part of nurturing. When you take the time to really, I mean *really*, relax, you will be able to recharge your body, mind, and soul. Many days I will go, go, go, and find that I am being bombarded with texts, phone calls, and emails. I feel like my life is chaos. But from using my balance habits, I remember to give myself some time, even if it's only a few minutes, to relax my face, neck, and shoulders, then move the relaxation feeling to my chest as I breathe, noticing my lower body also starting to relax as I breathe deep into my root chakra, and then bring all that relaxing and breathing back up into my stomach, then chest, then throat, and out my mouth.

This visualization technique of breathing while focusing on relaxing muscles is a fantastic way to center yourself and align with the universe. While you relax your body sitting comfortably in a chair, you can feel blessed and thankful for that comfortable chair. When you relax your heart, you can recall clearly all the love and joy already in your life. When you relax your mind like this, you are aligning yourself for clarity and expansion. Once you feel fully calm and composed, you can return to the busyness of the world, but with more energy, filled with determination, clear thinking, and gratitude. Just remember, there is always enough time to do what is important to nurture just you.

> *As we function in this consciousness of the*
> *oneness of the universe, we lift the thought of*
> *the world around us.*—Nona Brooks

As I read and ponder on the quote above, I get a wonderful feeling of being connected to the universe, and my daydreaming enters into a reality that points out, "If we can feel that connectedness, then we are actually altering the world with our thoughts. Oneness creates it so."

When you are having issues with work or any relationship, the first thing to do is practice visualization while meditating on the problem. If you start to feel a sense of inner peace and harmony, you will also begin to feel happier and more balanced, which can help you connect more meaningfully with your work or with a relationship that may have issues.

The problems in our relationships often serve as a mirror of our own disconnection from ourselves. If we can get closer and clearer with our own selves first, we can help to improve our interactions with others.

As we visualize ourselves with less tension and let go of negative thoughts about the situation, we will automatically feel lighter and happier. This feeling or vibrational frequency helps you to be more compassionate and loving, which in return will help the relationship to be more loving. When you first address your own imbalance or your disharmony with your own inner being, then you can start to develop the right mindset to improve all of your relationships.

Commitment to consistent personalized, healthy action will ultimately help you recognize life stressors and make choices that support the life you want to live. Nurturing yourself is one of the best ideas to help you stay in balance with your work and your play. It is also an important step in forgiving yourself or a thought that you may have had. Loving yourself instead of condemning yourself raises your vibration and helps to balance you with your inner self.

Here is a meditation you can read each morning:

> I entrust my healing to the flow of the universe within me. True healing is the return of my body, mind, and emotions to alignment and balance with the universe. It is the spiritual restoration of wholeness to all parts of my being. I am connected to the image and likeness of God in expression, so I know I can enter into a perfect stillness and meditation to renew my divine qualities that I was born into. My mind is quiet, my body is open and receptive, and the healing of the universe is now in this perfect moment shining forth and bringing me into harmony with perfect health. Health is my natural state of being, and I draw forth that life-giving power in me now. I smile with joy, giving visible evidence to the universe's healing energy within me.
>
> I am whole.
> I am free.

I am healed.

All is well, and so it is.

Henry David Thoreau wrote, "The question is not what you look at, but what do you see?" We all have different opinions based on our programming from all that we have experienced in our life. Psychology has come a long way since the fifties, sixties, and even the seventies. Science now shows that our subconscious brains form with thought from our environment, from our parents, from our classmates, from our teachers, and so on.

If you grew up with a lot of negativity in your life, your subconscious may still be programmed from all those thoughts and your responses to them. But the cool thing is, we can reprogram our thoughts, and our subconscious cannot tell the difference. It just focuses on what we focus on. When we change our thoughts about what we see, the things we see will literally change too. When we become pure in our hearts, we become perfect in our spiritual vision. It is then that the intellect falls back to the original purity and truth of the divine pattern or programming that we were all born into.

Science and psychology have proven that we are not born bad or with sin; we are born with love as all there is, and then we learn fear, we learn doubt, we learn scarcity thinking. Many of us, including myself, are taught very early that we are born into this world with original sin. But if we find the good in ourselves and love ourselves, we shall also find that we can see this divine pattern in others.

We can see what the Buddhist teaches: that man is basically good. As we align ourselves with the good of the universe, others will respond to the good in us. As we learn to love ourselves more deeply, the deepness will respond to the same depth. The universal spirit is made up of love and peace and belongs to every human who will believe, trust, and know. Then what we see will change.

Again, if you think about the statement from Thoreau that it's not what you look at but what you see, you can realize the truth as you look around each day. You can choose to be upset with what you lack, or you can choose to be amazed at all the abundance. You can be discouraged by how far you must go to fulfill your desires, or be proud in each moment of how much you have accomplished. You can choose to see all the differences between you and others with judgment, or you can embrace that we are all humans on our own journey.

Your life changes drastically with the choices you make each day, so remember that the universe is love, and you and everyone else are a part of this universal love. You are part of the all-ness, and so is everything else. You can see all the infinite potential in a world that works for everyone through the eyes of a loving universe, and then you will continue to grow.

> *All the powerful things in the world are invisible,*
> *like honor, character, love, and your own power to*
> *visualize and make dreams come true. They are all*
> *lights within you, casting their rays around you, so*
> *that you can find your way. Open your eyes with faith,*
> *so that you can see them.* —*Celia Caroline Cole*

Try this nurturing affirmation: "In this moment, I feel with every fiber of my being that the universe and I are one. I let go of worry, and I focus on the light within. I am whole and complete, with unlimited potential to develop and align with the universe and feel love that casts out fear. I am open to ideas that expand my sense of oneness with the universe and allow me to express more love and light in the world."

Gratitude for Your Body

Since we have learned that gratitude is the easiest way to align with the universe, having gratitude for your body is essential in nurturing yourself. As Thich Nhat Hanh put it, "Your body is your first home. Breathing in, you arrive in your body. Breathing out, you are home."

We live in a society where the majority of people are obsessed with the way their body looks. They compare themselves daily with models in magazines and people in movies, television commercials, and social media. Body obsession can lead to so much attention that behind it lies a constant fear: fear of being rejected, fear that if your body is not perfect it is a reflection of a flaw in your character or a lack of nurture or care.

With this fear, you can lose sight of all the amazing things your body does for you. If you look at your body differently, with gratitude instead of fear, astounding things can happen. You can improve in health, vitality, and happiness, and the way you look at your body will change.

Just think of all the amazing things that happen every day in your body. Think of every cell and how it functions. Think of how miraculously all your organs work to break down food to create energy, build strength, and provide exactly what you need to lead a healthy life, pay attention, and practice gratitude.

In *NeuroWisdom: The New Brain Science of Money, Happiness, and Success*, authors Mark Robert Waldman and Chris Manning PhD discuss how you can change negative thoughts and feelings to more positive feelings, which will boost your brain and give you more optimal performance in work and in life. They call this *self-nurturance*. I tried it, and it works miracles.

Here is how they explain it:

> Self-nurturance is a stress reducing strategy that is done through pleasant touch. If you can regularly hug yourself or massage yourself, you can feel more kindness and compassion for yourself. It will soothe the emotional and social centers of the brain. By stimulating the sensory pleasure circuits of the brain, and massaging yourself, it can treat a wide variety of psychological disturbances and can enhance your overall well-being.

They suggest trying this experiment now:

> Close your eyes and think of something that makes you feel anxious or worried. Now begin to gently and slowly explore your fingers, hands, and arms with a soft touch. Slow it down, really slow, and take about 60 seconds to explore your palms, then your scalp, and also your face. You will notice that your anxiety will disappear and the slower you go, the more you will be able to enter into a

meditational state with your inner being, in the present moment, free from doubts or worries.

The neuroscience explained in the book is simple: you cannot simultaneously focus on both a pleasurable and a painful stimulus in the same moment. The authors advise that if you are tired or pressured at work, just give yourself a minute of self-nurturance, and you will see that your focus and productivity will suddenly increase.

I tried this technique when I was having trouble sleeping, and a simple massage of my neck and scalp, along with rubbing my feet with lavender lotion, helped me to relax and not think of all the day's hectic activity that was going through my head. The authors say that simple pleasures like self-nurturance can turn off busy thoughts in your frontal lobe that often keep you awake. So, stretch and hug yourself! What a great way to connect to your inner being.

CHAPTER 6

Celebrating

*The more you praise and celebrate your life,
the more there is in life to celebrate. Oprah
and Lifeisabeautifuladventure.com*

Celebrating is the highest form of gratitude. When you align with the universe by celebrating yourself, celebrating an event, or celebrating another person, the joy that comes from it will give you the highest vibration in that special moment, and your focus on that joy will only attract more joy and happiness to you. "I don't have to chase extraordinary moments to find happiness—it's right in front of me," says Brené Brown. "When we see and feel celebration, we can find joy everywhere."

Joy and happiness need to happen within before we can get the results we want from the outside world. Celebrating little moments in life or big moments in life will help you be a bigger, better, more balanced you. Your brain doesn't work by saying, "I'll celebrate when something I want happens." It works by celebrating and giving gratitude first.

Finding joy in the moment—visualizing and feeling that the thing you desire has already happened—allows the part of your brain called R.A.S., short for Reticular Activating System, to experience it as true. When RAS experiences joy, celebration of life, and happiness, it filters in those feelings and helps you to see even more things in life to be grateful for. When you take the time to celebrate who you are, love the things in your life, and feel gratitude for this joy, the light will flood your entire being and attract even more of that joy to you.

My best celebrating is done with the joy of music in my life. I love to attend live concerts, because the feeling and vibration of the music with others in that moment is a unified way of celebrating life together. I always feel like we are all one organism connected to each other through instruments, lyrics, dancing, and the extreme feeling of joy and celebration of life together in that moment. What could you celebrate in this moment in your life?

Try this fun exercise: List all the things you have celebrated about yourself or celebrated with others. See how you feel inside after you've written them down. Try to carry that feeling in the moment and align yourself with the universe in celebration of who you are and where you are going. The focus on *why* will provide you with the answers of *how* and *when*. When we focus on our *why*, the *why* is like rocket fuel for our *how*. *Why* gives your life purpose, and when you have purpose, the *how* becomes easier.

Repeat this affirmation: "My body is a blessing, just as it is today. I love my body, and I am grateful for everything it provides for me to live life fully. I give thanks for my body temple."

We have talked through many chapters about how we can have better balance. Celebrating is the sixth step to help get that inner being in balance. Celebrating is actually appreciating. It is a way of being grateful.

There is actually a science behind celebrating. Scientists have shown that appreciation can literally alter the human heart and the molecular structure of your brain. Scientists have discovered that feelings of gratitude can actually change your brain, and feeling gratitude can also be a great tool for overcoming depression and anxiety.

Furthermore, scientists have discovered that the heart can send signals to the brain. That's something to think about every time we struggle with depression. Why are we constantly encouraged to take a prescription medication when so many mindfulness techniques are actually showing more promise?

Gratitude is a funny thing if you think about it. There are some people in this world who get a clean drink of water, or at least some food, or a worn-out pair of shoes, and they can be extremely grateful for these things.

Meanwhile, in America and some other countries, people complain about things instead of celebrating them.

Here's a simple exercise. Every morning when you wake up, think of three ways you will celebrate your day. Write them down. share them, and you will find that your day will be more about being grateful instead of complaining.

Celebrate life with singing. I have always been a singer, and I am sure you are too. My mother tells stories of me singing as a very small child, mainly for attention. But as I became older, at around age eleven, I asked for a guitar and started expressing myself with the chords and rhythm of strumming the strings along with my singing. This always helped raise my attitude about life in the present moment.

I continued to sing my praises in our small church, and then I sang in many pageants, receiving scholarships for college. Then I actually sang in a band. I never really had the goal of singing professionally or any dreams of becoming a star. I just sang because it made me feel good. Now, after many years, scientists are discovering that music and singing are very healing physically and, of course, mentally.

The actual act of singing is one of the easiest ways to raise the vibration of your body. It helps you to harmonize and align yourself with the universe. Singing is a pure act of celebration. It is also an act of sorrow. Sing a song of pure celebration.

Even though singing is a pure act of celebration, it is also an act of sorrow. When you sing, you are in universal vibration with a song. You can chant, hum, sing solo, sing with others, or just sing along with your radio, and you will be using the highest vibrations of celebrating life with appreciation for that moment. Harmonizing and singing will help bring your body's vibrations into alignment with the universe. It is so easy; just try and feel. It is pure love in action.

I love celebrating life as an adventure. When we live life as an adventure, we are believing our life is worth living. We are reminded that life is an incredible gift and are grateful just to be alive. Think about all the millions of electrical impulses coursing through your heart and brain. Every second, your muscles are rhythmically contracting and letting go subconsciously without any true effort on your part. When you feel your life is an awesome adventure and what it truly means to be a spiritual being having a human experience, you can use imagination to celebrate your life and envision infinite possibilities.

You can create harmony with the world, and the universe will respond with more excitement, attraction, beauty, and joy. It will give you more to celebrate and be grateful for the more you radiate joy and celebrate your life with joy and happiness Celebrating life is a catapult to raising your frequency. As your frequency is aligned with the universe, you will receive back more to celebrate. The more good you give out, the more good you will receive. But you must be open to receiving it. When you program your mind to say yes by using affirmations and feeling the joy and truth that it is your reality, your subconscious then says yes as well, and your desires will be manifested through joy and acceptance.

I begin my day with spiritual practices that align
me with the Universe. Gabriel Bernstein

It is easy to look at our lives and celebrate the things that make us feel blessed. And it is easy to look forward to the future when we are joyfully celebrating the goals we have achieved. Our efforts will give our goals meaning. Our goals, once achieved, will remind us how blessed we are to have them come true for us. The promise of a better future is in sight.

Anticipation and optimism are two things that come along with celebration. When you feel alive with eagerness and excitement for more good things to happen in your life, you are inviting more success at the same time. There is no room for fear or shrinking, because optimism and anticipation is on a higher frequency of energy, aligning with the universe that only wants good for us. Instead of just waiting for your future, you can visualize it right now, in the present, using the feeling of exhilaration, happiness, and celebration in the moment that will align you with the life of your dreams.

I wrote this poem one morning in 2011 when I was feeling joyful and blessed and wanted to celebrate my day:

Celebration of Life
Beauty of nature lifts
my thoughts above.

Beauty is the soul bounty,
sister of love.
Green leaves, purple
flowers, shapes of real
things, that give no thought
to death or to their next meal.
Sun, water, wind and
earth give without
ever knowing thoughts
of receiving an ego or clout.
The celebration of life continues.
No man can conflict
the results of a world of love and
the beauty of nature's gift.

CHAPTER 7

Expanding

*The meaning of life is to find your gift. The
purpose of life is to give it away. Pablo Picasso*

We already talked about believing and that your beliefs are your own. You don't have to impose them on others. Judging others for their beliefs only causes you to resist. Allow others to stand their own ground, and you stand for yours. No hostility is needed.

In Brené Brown's book *The Gift of Imperfection*, she writes, "Whenever I'm faced with a vulnerable situation, I get deliberate with my intentions by repeating this to myself: 'Don't shrink. Don't puff up. Stand your sacred ground.'" This mantra can help when you are faced with others.

When we're focused on giving our gift to the world, the universe responds by opening doors and providing the necessary education for our enfoldment. Every time I have shared my gift with others through my workshops and seminars, I am open to receiving the gratitude that others feel when they have either learned something new about themselves or shared the lesson they learned with others. This I feel is the eternal process of forever expanding the finite. Focus on giving and be open to receiving.

Expand your thoughts, expand your mind, expand your heart. Albert Einstein challenged us to expand our hearts by "widening our circle of compassion, to embrace all living creatures and the whole of nature in its beauty." While this may not align with how the world says we should conduct ourselves, I challenge you to extend or expand your kind deeds to even those who are not always pleasant to be around or are not so easy to love.

Compassion is a wonderful tool for expanding your heart to be less judgy. Open your heart to people who are different from you. There is no one or no thing that has not been created in the love of the all-loving, all-knowing universe. We are all connected, so when you judge, you bring up a resistance, and that resistance will stop you from receiving and will stop you from expanding to your highest good.

I was raised to judge because the God that was taught to me was a judging God. I have since learned that judgment of a situation or of a person is only based on fear—fear of not having enough and, most of all, fear of doing wrong. *Who am I to judge?* is now my mantra. The freedom that comes from this daily affirmation has caused my heart to open up and receive.

There is a power for good in the universe greater
than you are ... Learn to use it!—Ernest Holmes

In his book *This Thing Called Life*, Ernest Holmes said it so eloquently: "We have all been trying to find out just what our relationship to life is, because we know by pure intuition that we could establish a right relationship with the invisible, we should find peace, health, harmony, prosperity and happiness. We can live in the kingdom of heaven, while on earth."

Having your inner being in balance and being your most authentic self expands your alignment with the universe to create the life of your dreams. As Ernest Holmes wrote, "I am strong and free through the action of spirit in me. I am well and successful in everything I do."

If thinking of troubles will double the size, then sheer
logic would show it to be more wise, to try the same
system on Blessings and such, we might be astonished
that they'd also swell so much.—Shirley Boyes

Spirit, according to Ernest Holmes, can be defined as "the invisible life and intelligence underlying all physical things."

Pandemic Insights

As I write this book, we are in the thirty-fifth day of the stay-at-home order due to the COVID-19 pandemic. Some people want their state to reopen, and some people say it's too soon. I am personally frustrated and feel that we should reopen, but then my heart goes out to the people who have lost loved ones or those who have underlying conditions that make them worry that the coronavirus could kill them.

When I feel frustrated by personal or even professional challenges (I want to get back to work) or feel unsafe or concerned about a situation or event, I have learned to seek a greater understanding. The best way to do this is just to open my heart and listen. I can gather more information about the subject or event by asking questions or request the advice of someone I trust.

Unless we are constantly expanding our thought,
we are not growing.—Ernest Holmes.

If I am ever in conflict with someone over a difference of opinion, I practice understanding with a curious mind and an open heart. What happens next is usually an open heart from the other person. When I let down my resistance to the subject or event, spiritual truth begins to illuminate my consciousness. I can stand firm in love instead of fear, and I am guided by this truth of spiritual understanding. My frustrations are replaced by more knowledge and safety. I understand more fully the fear of the people who want to stay home and not reopen the economy due to the virus, and this allows more love to help them. My mantra is, "Remove negative thoughts. Relax your state of mind. Recharge your body."

The gift of heaven is forever made. The receiving
of this gift is an eternal process of forever
expanding the finite.—Ernest Holmes

When I commit to expressing my higher self, my true authentic personality emerges. But there is always room for improvement. I begin by becoming more aware of my judgments and also listening to what others are saying, because we all have different experiences in life and also different gifts. During the COVID-19 pandemic, I became very aware of the way people reacted to the virus. There are many different opinions—political, scientific, and even spiritual. I am being shown how important it is to recognize the good in all people, even though I disagree with a lot of the opinions surrounding the fear of the disease.

Fear is the absence of love. I personally don't fear the disease, so my reaction toward it has been very peaceful and loving. I have been able to meditate on the healing of people who have been diagnosed with the disease as well as the medical personnel who are working to help heal those same people. I have used this world event to explore my inner journey and expand my understanding of my own spiritual nature.

When I see or read something about the way the disease is being handled by fearful thinking, I am making a commitment to not judge and at the same time exploring my higher self. I let my divine nature guide me in all that I say and do. Every move I make, every step I take along this path of self-exploration is a step to better express who I am. I am learning to value and understand the knowledge and different perspectives that others can bring to our united experience of being in this pandemic, all connected in this experience of life.

I have come to realize that I didn't publish this book before COVID-19 existed because my gift to the world of teaching how to master balance in life would not have been discussed. This major experience has touched almost everyone in the world. It is truly a historical event, and I am sharing it with billions of people. I feel grateful that I can lovingly share my gifts with the world, and in doing so, I am blessed. Wishing is an example of praying, which is an example of affirming.

Let's Talk About Miracles

Miracles are things that happen that are out of the ordinary. I celebrate my miracle moments, and so can you. Miracle moments actually are happening all the time, but we get so wrapped up in our daily work and responsibilities that the majority of people don't even notice them. Here are a few of my miracle moments. Once received, those miracles guide me to gratitude. And like I said before, gratitude is a clear form of celebrating the good in your life.

> *When we ask for anything, we are to believe that*
> *we already have it, but we are to ask only for that*
> *which is in unity with life.—Ernest Holmes*

We all have spiritual authority over our own life. We need to use it. Just stay aligned with the universe and believe. You can call forth the good that you desire by standing strong in your conviction. Know and believe that you can move mountains.

Repeat this affirmation: "I speak my word with spiritual authority, knowing that my desires come true, as I believe."

> *To meet everything and everyone through stillness*
> *instead of mental noise is the greatest gift you*
> *can offer the universe.—Eckhart Tolle*

We all know the feeling of being out of balance when we have too much work to do and never-ending commitments, yet some people can be truly healthy and happy with little down time. When I was in my twenties, this was how I felt—like I could conquer anything and everything with no downtime. But remember my story, working in New York for the famous Fashion Designer: after ten years of living like that, I became very ill.

While there is nothing wrong with having a busy business and loving what you do, there are times where you may overextend yourself and need to try expanding on simplicity versus expanding on growth. The word *business* can be too much *busyness!* Try gaining some equilibrium and inner balance before adding something new to your packed calendar of events. This happens by establishing limits. Decide what you will and will not do based on your personal and professional priorities.

Determine where your priorities fit on your calendar and make sure it's not all obligations for work, leaving you with little personal downtime. Just start with a list or outline, writing down personal health and well-being, including relaxation. Then, on another list, put everything else that you do not feel passionate about. There may be things you are adding to your life and work that are unnecessary. Start to prioritize with these lists what is most important to you and expand on those activities.

By using this prioritizing of events as to what is most important for your inner being in balance, you can start to simplify your life and get rid of the pressure to do it all. Try looking at the situation that may be causing you stress about completing or doing and then just say no. When we say *yes* to so many obligations, we can easily get off balance with what we truly want. Your willingness to simplify your life is another step toward growing as an individual and taking control of your life.

Try looking at and imagining each new commitment you are being asked to do and how it will impact your life if you say yes. I am learning this myself every day as I grow. I believe you will learn to simplify your life as well by expanding your thoughts on simplification versus trying to do it all.

Try this expanding consciousness exercise: Every time you walk through a doorway—whether in your home, in your car, on a bus or other modes of transportation, or at your workplace, say these words to yourself: "'I am blessed as I enter heaven." Try to feel heaven as a state of energy, a state of expanded consciousness. Visualize and realize how we can make decisions in our life that can be less *me* and more *we*.

How can we create a better world for people in the future? Sustainability and stability can create a balance for the planet and its inhabitants to align with oneness and interconnectedness. Whenever I have challenges or decisions that I must make, this is when it is most important to align myself with the universe. I have learned to step back and look objectively at my choices and then ask for guidance.

My outlook on how I want things to go, is created by shifting my awareness to the positive side of things, and I can begin to see outcomes clearly as they are, which is my truth. I become intuitively connected to the universe, and I allow myself to see the answers. I am directed to do what I know is right. My vision becomes clear as I shift my focus and awareness to see all things new. I am comforted knowing that I have choices, and I can always bring trust into any decisions I make. That trust always aligns me with my highest good.

Just remember these words: "Life isn't happening *to* me; life is happening *through* me." Looking around, I can see order is a constant in the universe. I can see all the patterns of growth in flowers and plants and note the rhythm of the seasons, the sun and moon, and the tides. There is a perfection in the flow of the universe, just like my life can be joined with this same perfection. I can notice times in my life where I tried to push for a certain outcome, and I just need to remember that the divine order and right action is always at work in any situation. How I think, feel, and act in response to everything that comes my way creates the life I live.

This belief is a very important step in allowing. We talked about how important allowing is to manifesting. Once we allow our divine connection to expand to the universe, it will guide us in the right action, and the life we create is our true authentic purpose for living. Faith and trust become part of every decision you make, and life happens through you.

> *Every new beginning starts at another new*
> *beginning's end.—Anonymous*

I expand my thinking by visualizing the path I am on and the desire of something that I want to receive. What I have learned and want to share with you reading this book, is how to keep expanding on your thoughts by visualizing the outcome. When you have a desire, you must go ahead and prepare to receive it. Start lining up the things you will need and get ready for the outcome. These types of actions signal the universe that you are ready to receive. You are serious about your intentions, and the universe is listening. You will start receiving creative ideas and meaning, to bring that desire into manifestation. Your balance and alignment with the universe is, a pure manifestation of living the life of your dreams.

> *The divine operation is always for expansion and fuller*
> *expression, and this means the production of something*
> *beyond what has gone before, something entirely new, not*
> *included in past experience, though proceeding out of it*
> *by an orderly sequence of growth.—Thomas Troward*

> *No matter how much good we experience today,*
> *the universe has more in store for us tomorrow. We*
> *should joyfully look forward to this expansion with*
> *enthusiastic anticipation.*—Ernest Holmes

> *In the great unity of all life, when you have*
> *a need, the answer is already moving on its*
> *way toward you.*—Eric Butterworth

All things come to us through our thoughts. I have discussed this concept throughout this book. My chapter on expanding is about how we can use our thoughts to grow and become our bigger and better selves and be in better balance. Growth is the law of life and is truly necessary to grow and expand your thinking. We cannot stand still; our mind is a muscle, and it can atrophy just like any other muscle in the body if it is not used and exercised.

We must get over the old idea of limitation. We can set ourselves up for miracles. We must dare to be great, and great things will happen. By expanding our thoughts and making ourselves the biggest and best selves that we can be, we will allow our dreams to become a reality.

When you are expanding your thought with visualization and seeing the things that you desire are already true and already existing in your life, your reticular activating system will focus on it and will continue to focus on it, and you will have the power to notice these ideas coming into your life. You will meet the perfect person to help you with your new idea. Synchronicity will take its place in your life and in your business, and it will grow and expand the more you visualize it as so.

It only takes thirty seconds a day in the morning to use visualization for expanding your thoughts. Your brain will be programmed for you to notice and attract what you need to achieve to cause a miracle. There is so much discomfort, sickness, and death with this COVID-19 pandemic, but we can transform it into something more beautiful. Once we transform this worldly event, those of us who trust in divine intervention will flourish and have wings to lift us from chaos and fear. We will expand our own divinity and truly make the world a better place to live, because we know that nature is giving us another chance.

Meditation and Mindfulness

Another wonderful way to expand your energy every day to align with the universe is with some sort of meditation or mindfulness. Since meditation is an art that balances the entire body, your chakra system (different energy points in the body that align from your tailbone to the top of your head) opens your inner being to love, peace, and harmony. There are many different forms of meditation, and I have found that walking meditation, guided meditation, and crystal meditation help me to focus my awareness with the present moment. Any method you choose to expand your mindfulness with meditation offers you the potential to reach a state of inner-being enlightenment.

What I personally like about meditation is that it is a pure way to connect to the highest source of energy, and it is not tied to any particular religion. It can be done anywhere at any time during your day, and with practice, it will enable spiritual development to take place along with scientific proof that new thoughts and new cellular development is happening with your brain as well as healing your mind and body.

Meditation is not a quick fix. It takes lots of practice, and it is truly an art form that takes some time to learn. But when practiced over a period of time, science has shown that it brings amazing benefits, such as a higher frequency of energetic awareness of how to heal certain ailments or diseases for yourself and for others. It has been proven that meditation lowers a person's blood pressure and helps calm the mind from stressful and chaotic emotions. It has also been proven that with at least twenty minutes of meditation a day, your focus becomes clearer on what your desires are, and you can align your energy to achieve success.

In her book *Crystals*, Jennie Harding explains how using crystals as a focus for mediation is easy and has major health benefits, as well as how applying this simple practice into your life every day helps with attracting what you want and desire your life to look like. She explains that since everything has energy and it cannot be created or destroyed, "using a crystal during mediation, is where the energy of the crystal itself, contributes to the experience. You can choose any crystal and can choose by being drawn to a stone for its color, shape, or feel. You may read about a stone and decide you want to work with it. You may simply look at your collection, and feel that particular piece jumps out at you."

Harding goes on to explain two simple ways to meditate with a crystal, gem, or stone:

> The first is to gaze at it. Mediation with eyes focusing on an object, is a technique from Zen tradition, where contemplation stills the mind. With a lit candle beside you, let your eyes rest on the stone and focus on it as long as you can without looking away from it. If you need to, you can look at the candle for a brief moment, then back at the stone. Notice any thoughts, feelings, or impressions that come to you and then let them float away. After twenty minutes, write notes to recall any important details.

The second way to meditate with a crystal, gem, or stone, Harding writes, is for maintaining balance:

> Hold the crystal in your left hand, and cover it with your right. The left hand is receptive and the right hand is dynamic, and by holding the crystal between them this way, the yin and yang balance of energy is maintained. Relax, close your eyes, and breathe calmly. Simply let your mind rest and focus on the stone between your hands. Notice how it feels and how you feel. You may notice sensations of warmth or tingling in your hands or elsewhere in the body. After breathing deeply and coming out of the mediation, make notes of any important impressions.

I have a personal testimonial of how crystals can heal by using them to balance, ground, and cleanse the energy frequencies of a disease in your body. During my two years of healing my Graves' disease, I went to a well-known healer in the Denver metro area, Dannie Huggs, who uses crystals to lay in the energy fields on the body where the disease had caused low frequencies.

It has been scientifically proven that disease in your body causes low impulses in the area that is being affected by the disease. Mine was the thyroid area of my neck and my heart, as well as my stomach, because the thyroid controls all the endocrine aspects of the body, including digestion and metabolism. My heart rate was very high, and I had lost twenty-five pounds in less than six months due to my thyroid being out of balance.

Dannie used crystals and stones that she believed could heal my disease, based on the energy that they held for certain areas or *layouts* of the body and the chakra points. She placed one on my forehead between my eyes, the third eye or the indigo chakra energy point that helps with intuition and inner knowing. Then she laid one on my neck, right where my thyroid is located; this is the blue chakra point, for expression and your voice. Another stone was placed on my heart, the green chakra energy point, for love and compassion (she said I needed to have more love for myself and to quit judging the disease). The last stone was placed on my stomach, the yellow chakra energy point for balancing my solar plexus, which is the energy involved with digestion and all the vital organs involved with digestion.

I went away from this session with clearer vision, a desire to heal myself, and a more relaxed and balanced feeling of love and compassion for myself and this so-called autoimmune disease that had taken over my body. I purchased the stones that the healer had used on my body, and I performed the same ritual every morning for thirty days. As I mentioned earlier in the book, I was also getting balanced through acupuncture. I changed my diet to include healing foods for this disease and avoid foods that had too many of the nutrients I already had in my system, which could cause an increase in production the T3 and T4 hormones. These had been shown through my bloodwork to be the reason for my disease and essentially my imbalance.

I slowly began to gain weight. I easily visualized being a healthy person using these stones with meditation, and my love and compassion for myself increased every day that I meditated on the healing of this disease that had no cure. As you know from reading earlier, I have been in complete remission for three years and deeply appreciate the disease that I learned so much about myself from having. I am truly blessed and appreciate all the healers in my life who helped me balance my seven points of energy fields as well as taught me the art of using crystals to meditate.

I now use crystals during walking meditation. My family and some close friends built a labyrinth in the front yard of my second home in Grand Lake, Colorado. The love, strength, and sweat that went into building this sacred place for a walking meditation fills it with joy and compassion. There is a picture of it on the back of this book. Taking crystals in my hands and holding them while walking slowly with contemplation and intention for my desires, I have manifested many dreams into reality.

This is one of the most amazing and easy meditations you can do. It only takes about five minutes. By setting aside this small amount of time each day, using a walking meditation, and focusing on your breath, you can still your mind and get into a Zen feeling of pure awareness of the present moment.

When you are ready and willing to learn a wonderful way to easily meditate, then use the Seven Chakra system power points, along with special meanings, and there is a color associated with each power point. Just expand and focus on that particular color, so that you can use this to help you with your meditation practice and expand your awareness.

The Seven Chakras

The first one is the Root Chakra. It is based right at the end of your tailbone. It is the foundation of the entire Charka system and you can meditate sitting and starting at your root chakra area. The color is red signifying love, power and energy. Focus on the point with the color red to help you with strengthening or energizing yourself, but is mostly associated with grounding yourself.

The Sacral Chakra, it is located right below your navel. This Charka symbolizes the area where you experience emotions and where creative derives. The center point for sexuality and pleasure. Focus here if you want to enhance your creativity and balance your emotions. The color for your Sacral power point is orange.

The Solar Plexus Charka, located at your navel and has a powerful beat from your heart, and you can feel it beat in that area of your body. It is the power and wisdom Charka. The area to focus for confidence, opinions and beliefs. Think about fire and the color yellow for the sun too. Focus here is you want to ignite your inner being and access your gut instinct, put Yellow energy around your Solar Plexus area.

The Heart Chakra is the fourth power point. It is located at the center of your chest. The color is green and the energy point is all about transformation, love, beauty, empathy and compassion. You can focus on your Heart Chakra when you need to forgive of if you want to experience appreciation. This Charka also radiates your inner being intentions, making this an energy point for manifesting your heart's desires and everything that you want in your life, so focus on love and the color green. And use for mediation on relationships.

The firth power point is the Throat Charka. It is located in the area above your chest and below your chin, your entire throat area. It is in charge of communication and helping you speak your truth without fear and your life purpose and your expression, creativity and your authentic voice. The Throat Chakra and the color blue is how to put your focus on when you are visualizing the gateway to true freedom and happiness.

When your throat Chakra is all aligned with your whole inner being, you can discover your most authentic self and show the world that you are living with your purpose and passion. It is easy to meditate and focus on the color blue, use blue crystals as a focus of blue energy too.

The Sixth Chakra is called the Third Eye. This energy point is all about perception and is located between your eyebrows and is directly related to the pineal gland in your brain, which is in charge of sleep, dreams and intuition. The color associated is indigo. Which is a wonderful color to use with visualization and as a power tool for having deep meditation. It is the area of the third eye, that can help you to manifest your own guidance and intuition. You can achieve balance in your inner being, by listening to it in silence, seen and unseen then perceive the lesson of it all. Use your third eye as a power point for great meditation. Ask and it is given.

The seventh and final Chakra is the Crown. It is located at the top of the head and you can think of it as a crown for your highest self. Think of the soft spot that each of us was born with. This is the energy point that connects us to the Universe and to all living creatures. It helps take you from thoughts of your own self and your own needs, to the needs of others. Focus on this Crown Chakra when you want to work towards expanding your highest self, to connect to something bigger. This charka color is violet and turns to a bright white, as we allow the access, alignment and balance, with all your other chakras. This will help your inner being to be in tune with the wisdom, beyond the sensory realm.

I encourage you to use the seven Chakra system when you are trying to meditate. You can start with the Root Chakra and go up to the crown Chakra and sense your energy along each point and move straight up the balanced path and allow that white light to leave the crown and go out into the Universe. I have an easy way to remember the colors, but I can't remember who told me it was so, so, long ago. But we used the name, Roy G. Biv. It is an easy way to try and remember the colors and the order of the 7 aligned chakras points.

Red

Orange

Yellow

Green

Blue

Indigo

Violet

I encourage you to try all these techniques on how to meditate and expand your life, expand your business and keep expanding beyond.

You might be reading this and saying to yourself, *This, is all a bunch of woo-woo stuff that could never work for me*. Well, this all comes back to your believing, allowing, learning, affirming, nurturing, and then expanding on how it could work for you, with the result of balancing your inner being. Like I wrote earlier, instead of saying, "I will believe it when I see it," say "I will see it when I believe it."

Let's get a little more scientific so that you can understand and learn more about how our brain works with color. As you know, there is a seven-color spectrum of the rainbow, and there are seven colors of the body's chakra energy points in the body. Each of these colors can be seen with your eyes. The main rays of a rainbow are red, orange, yellow, green, blue, indigo, and violet.

The eyes allow color to be perceived and interpreted by the brain.

So, in essence, color can influence how we feel and react in our everyday experiences. Jennie Harding explains the world of color and how we see it by discussing the structure of the eyes:

> Each eye is a small, roughly spherical structure that is about 1 inch in diameter. The remainder of the eye's surface is set back inside the skull. The eyes connect to optical nerves that relay the impressions of light back to the brain, particularly and area in the back of the brain call the visual cortex, where visual impressions are interpreted.
>
> Inside each eyeball are a number of important structures. There is a lens that becomes thinner when you look into the distance or thicker when you look close up. The iris, the colored part of the eye, is actually a muscle that changes size of the pupil in order to control the amount of light entering the eye. At the back of the eye is the retina, a layer with two types of light sensitive cells called rods and cones. The rods help us see in darkness and distinguish black, white, and shades of gray; the cones enable us to see red, green, and blue, and are better suited to detecting fine detail in daylight.

I don't know about you, but I find this extremely interesting. Being able to see color is one of the most miraculous gifts of the human body, and it adds such immense variety to our daily lives.

For millions of years, as we have evolved, our eyes and our brains have changed and developed for the purpose of interpreting color. When you look and feel red, orange, and yellow, do you have feelings of warmness? These three colors in our chakra system are located in the core of the body where heat is generated and can have a stimulating and energizing effect. Just imagine the colors of a fire. Greens, blues, and violets are cooler hues that can have a soothing effect. Imagine a calm lake of blue water.

Nature is best at providing color therapy for us, as well as the colors of crystals and stones. Think of the outside and how nature can provide us with blue skies surrounded by green trees. If you really think about how life was before the invention of the electric light, it was governed and dictated by the sun during the day and the moon during the night. The effects of the light and the spectrum of these seven colors in nature have been a part of human nature since the beginning of time.

Now that we have the invention of light, our brains and eyes can interpret so much more, and we can learn to use them for healing and balancing our inner world as well as our outer world. It is really up to you in what you want to believe and utilize in your life with colors you see and how they make you feel. I, for one, am a believer, and the miracles that have happened in my life, based on trusting nature, along with colors of the spectrum and chakra system, have healed more than disease for me. They have enhanced every aspect of every day in my physical and spiritual life.

My personal thoughts on this COVID-19 situation that I am facing is that I am divinely protected. Nothing can harm me, because I am shielded by the universal spirit's loving care. I remember this truth when I am vulnerable and exposed. I am comforted to know that this divine power is always within me and around me. No matter what is happening in my environment or in my relationships, it cannot touch me.

I repeat soothing and powerful affirmations at times when I may feel afraid or anxious. We are faced with living with the unknown with this pandemic, but what I do know is that if I stay focused, centered, and balanced with the alignment of the universe and its divine presence, I will be protected. I have confidence that this alignment will help guide me to the divine truth: that all is well in my world.

Expanding Your Inner Being

In any given moment, we have two options: to step forward into growth or step back into safety. What one can be, one must be. We never know what's inside us until we face our fears and move through them, pushing through resistance, trepidation, and doubts to claim our personal power.

How can we have a more expansive life? Ernest Holmes writes, "Life is a song, let's sing it!" If we allow life to be a song, we must invite the song in. Emerson speaks of the stars and if they came out every hundred years, we would look up and marvel at such a sight. But since they come out every night, many people hardly notice them. It's easy to let the day run you instead of you running your own day, and then all the world becomes very trivial.

Every day when we awake, we can expand on how we want the day to go and ask ourselves, "What brought me the most joy today? Where was I most alive?" William James put it like this: "These then are my last words to you. Be not afraid of life. Believe that life is worth living, and your belief will help create the fact."

I love this simple story that can help us relate to having more clarity in life: A young couple moves into a new neighborhood, and at the breakfast table one morning, the wife notices that the neighbor's wash hanging outside looks like it is not clean.

The wife says to her husband, "Maybe they need to use better soap!"

This conversation goes on for several mornings, until one day the wife looks out and says, "The clothes look clean now. I guess the neighbors have changed their soap?"

The husband replies, "No, I got up early this morning and washed our windows."

What a great example of how we judge things by their appearance. That is how life is; what we see in others often depends on the clarity in our own lives.

As we are growing in our spirituality and expanding our alignment with the universe, we can remove obstacles that block our true potential. It's just like when you walk into a dark room; you can strike a match or just flip a switch, and the dark room will become a room full of light. If a lamp is turned off, we know that there is electricity and we can choose to turn the lamp on again. Even though we may have obstacles in life that will challenge us and block our light, we know there is still a choice, and the source of light is still constant and available to us.

The universe and/or spirit is present in every person, place, and situation, even if we can't see it. When we are faced with a situation where we believe we can't live through it and we are judging it as negative or bad, we are creating it as an obstacle that can block the light. Since we all have freedom to choose what we want to focus on, it is as easy as flipping a switch, choosing to shift our attention to the light, seeing a situation as positive, and connecting with the universe for the right action and guidance. Choosing to be in alignment with your highest self will remove any obstacles blocking your way, and the darkness will dissolve. Maintaining a conscious awareness of this connection to your higher self helps you to remain in the light.

Every loss, every hardship, every painful event provides us with an opportunity to grow. We just need to be open to receiving the lesson. We can learn from the experience and get to work on our future. Life doesn't stay the same. Security in life is never 100 percent secure. If we don't take risks in life, we will never learn.

Columbia University researchers found that when a person is learning something new, age has nothing to do with it. Whether they were fifteen years old or seventy-five, people were able to learn a new language or a new piece of technology. The only time older people had difficulty learning something new was when they used age as an excuse.

Life will always meet our expectations of it. Our consciousness mirrors our thoughts, and our life will be how we see it internally and externally. There is a wonderful story about a man sitting by the side of the road near the entrance to a small town. He greets another man who is moving to this town, and the stranger asks, "What are people like in this town?"

The man asks the stranger, "What were the people like in your last town?"

The stranger replies, "Cold and unkind."

"Then people here will be the same," the man replies.

A few minutes later, another stranger happens by and asks the same question. Once again, the man asks what the people were like in his last town.

"Wonderful, loving, and kind," says the stranger.

"I suspect that is what you will find here," the man answers.

From this story, we learn that what we expect from life is what we will get. Wherever you are in life, you can change what life is bringing you by changing your pattern of thinking. Change how you see something and the thing you see will change. Expand your thinking so that your life will expand.

Expand on how you have invited "allowing" into your life. When you allow the universe to align with your path of least resistance, you will discover that life becomes easy. Your goals and dreams for your future begin to come true because you are allowing the good that has already been created to enter in and manifest. When you elevate and expand with the step of allowing, your true purpose in life will be easily exposed to you, and you will begin to feel like you are in the flow of life. Your physical body will become lighter, and your mind will feel freer. Being less judgmental lessens resistance, and soon, negative thoughts will become a thing of the past. Only expand on your positive thinking and allow your thoughts to become true.

After reading this book, ask yourself again: what does it mean to you, to live with inner balance? My belief is that in order to obtain inner balance, we have three distinct things to align: the mind, the body, and the spirit. Balancing these three is the key to living a whole, happy, and complete life.

Every day, I seek balance between work and family, between my needs and desires and those of the ones I love and also between my responsibilities and relaxation. There are days when I feel pulled in different directions, but I have learned that I can have a choice. I can stop and focus and breathe into that moment and find clarity in weighing my options and moving forward mindfully, with purpose and intention.

Every day, I affirm that my mind, body, and spirit are in alignment with my life. I realize that I am happy, whole, and complete. I am grateful. I remember that I can create whatever day I want to receive, and I allow for stability and order to exist by spending the time needed to meditate, engage with friends and family, and participate in sports or hobbies. I can visualize balance and beauty in my life and know that it is up to me to create the balance. No one else decides this for me. I know that I have a choice to be in alignment with the universe to allow resistance against it. My choice is to be a whole, balanced, and complete being.

Holy Harmony

Once we have inner balance, we are in alignment with the universe. If we as humans can practice daily to let go and let god (any name you want to call it—being, light, spirit, mother nature, etc.), then we will be allowing our true nature to guide us. We can learn to be more intuitive, with objective responses to our worldly challenges.

As Eckhart Tolle writes in his book *The Power of Now*, thinking and doing too much and not spending enough time just being has caused an epidemic of people living with depression, anxiety, and helplessness. When we turn over our thoughts and decisions to our higher selves while in a quiet solitude of "no thinking," then no-thing can lead us astray. We can be in total holy harmony.

Remember what Marianne Williamson was quoted saying at the beginning of my book? Life is all about Metaphysical Principles. The Power of Spirit is inside of us. It's called our Inner Being. It is not outside of us.

When we feel separate from others, we are not living our deepest truth. We are actually disempowering ourselves.

Also, the Ultimate Truth is; there is no time or space. This is a part of the human Illusion. There is no place where you start and where I finish. We are all connected to the same reality. Ernest Holmes says, "You can only achieve what you can conceive." On the Spiritual Realm, there is no give and take, there is just giving and receiving. So, what I believe is; you must be open to receiving.

When you wake up in the morning, expand your awareness by asking these questions to your Inner Being;

"How can I be the highest and best today?"

"What would you have me do?"

"Who would you have me meet?"

Enlightenment is a journey of responding positively to everything that happens in your life. Miracles don't happen in the past; they happen in the present. Anytime, the mind is not used in the present, the programming of your future will happen no matter what, so live in the now, and miracles will happen. Our only experience on earth that is real, is to "give love and receive love". Don't get attached to outcomes, just be present and positive with faith and a belief that, "All is Well."

In living authentically with a growth and an intentional mindset; we are creating things from the inside out. People will like you and want to do business with you, because of your positivity and they can feel it. It's not just about your Resume', it's about who you really are. People will see your value and want to work with you.

How can you be your most authentic self? Follow your Inner Being and have it in balance with the 7 principles I have discussed in this book. Once you learn your purpose, share your truth. Remember, an idea is stronger when it is shared. Find something in life where you can be of service and share your beliefs. Be aware. Be of value. Be You.

As I am finishing up this book, the world is in a never-before situation called the coronavirus pandemic. The last time anything similar happened was in 1918, when the Spanish flu killed 33 million people on this planet. My family and I, along with people in 40 other states in our nation, are being told to stay home, physically distance from others, wear masks over our faces, and close businesses that are not "essential" to try to keep people from gathering. Emotions of fear and anger have been erupting due to people losing their jobs, scarcity of medical supplies, and the unknown of this virus and the impact it is having on our lives.

My intuition and emotions from the beginning have been of peace, not fear—just divine guidance leading me to explore all the opportunities in this situation and being in the present moment. I am learning new technology to help me stay connected to the outer world, since we cannot gather for my workshops and classes. I am meditating more than I have ever done, and I am trusting myself with my feelings of encouragement that our world is going to be an even better place once this pandemic is over and us humans start again with a fresher and newer concept of how we should live. Nature is showing us that we must change, since we are part of nature and our species is all connected. We are finding ourselves in a situation where we must care for each other. We must put love over fear in order to survive.

Many great teachers, like Abraham Hicks, Marianne Williamson, Deepak Chopra, and Dr. Joe Dispenza, have been reaching out through social media to help others feel that love is the answer. The more love and forgiveness our universe provide, the closer we are as humans to recognizing our spiritual nature and seeing the truth of this situation. It has been said more than once by these spiritual leaders that our planet is in the cocoon phase of transformation. Nature is showing us that in order to become a butterfly, we must first struggle and move through the growth period. I have discovered from the stay-at-home order during the coronavirus pandemic that I am facing my fears of what happens next. We are all living in the unknown.

The unknown has always frustrated me, and when I get frustrated, I get stressed. When I get stressed, I get migraines. This is when I must face my fears and step into my personal power. I stop and take a look at why I am allowing resistance. The resistance is what causes my migraines. I have to look at my diet. I have to look at my breathing.

When I stop and listen to my breathing, I begin to notice that I am not breathing and taking in enough oxygen, which can trigger migraines, just like sugar can trigger migraines. I know then that my practice of being in the moment is not happening. I stop in that moment and breathe. I rely on the power of the now to heal my migraines. No past thoughts and no future thoughts, just the power of the moment, breathing in and letting breath out. I allow the path of least resistance to take over, and then my stress is relieved. I am healed.

I am excited and fulfilled that I finished my book on inner being in balance, so that I can help others live to their full potential, discover their freedom, and see that whatever their true selves are wishing for can be achieved. My life, like that of others, has been full of challenges, but after discovering that I can manifest the life I truly love by taking action toward making the balance a reality, I can now help others do the same. If you are still reading this, you now have the secret to manifesting all your desires.

Maintaining inner being balance is the first step to staying on the right and true path to success. Inner being in balance is an art form. Inner being in balance is freedom. Inner being in balance is expansion that connects us all together. Inner being in balance is love.

I hope you will practice the seven principles to manifesting an inner being in balance. I would love to see you align with the universe to manifest the life of your dreams. Please know that I am thinking of you and I am connected to you. We are all in this world together, and we are all connected to the highest source of the universe. Its' energy is a part of our own energy. As I send love to you, I will feel the love that you send back to me.

Let's all practice the visualization of our planet being healed. And with that expanding thought, we will have inner peace.

Namaste
Monica Graves

Acknowledgements

I am beyond grateful for the many people in my life, who helped make this book a reality. The first, big thanks, would be my husband, Michael Graves, who believed in me from the beginning 5 years ago when I started this journey to write a book and he actually typed up my 15 years of journaling, because I can only freestyle handwrite and nothing was typed!

My sons, Baron and Gunner, who also believed in me, have given much love and support, and some great stories to tell in the book.

I am so blessed to have a big loving family, who always loves me unconditionally and accepts me for who "I AM."

Thank you to Patricia Crane and Rick Nichols for the Louise Hay Training. You are wise masters of Louise Hay Philosophy. I am grateful to be a certified Heal Your Life Teacher. A lot of learning and a lot of love!

A big shout out to Larry Kendall, the author of "Ninja Selling", who as a person and mentor, changed my life and business completely in 2011.

Thank you to John Assaraf, who I haven't met personally, but I joined his Neurogym coaching for life and for business, he has taught me so much about the brain and how to recondition it for the better. John's book, "The Answer: Grow any Business, Achieve Financial Freedom, and Live an Extraordinary Life, is a reference book for my life and business, and I read it often.

Thank you to Lon Welsh, the owner of Your Castle Real Estate Brokerage, where I work. He has given me the freedom to teach, to consult, to write, to build my real estate empire, and has been my accountability partner for 11 years!

Thank you to all the many teachers, therapists, and healers I have met along the way. I really don't know what direction my life would have led to, if I had not met and learned such profound teachings. Now, to give back, I am sharing what I have learned from you, in this book.

I also want to thank all my gal pals, and believe me, I have an abundance of them. Each of them has contributed to my life in so many ways. You have made me who I am, because of the love we share, and all the experiences we have shared together, over so many years.

Finally, I need to give more thanks to Michael, my soulmate, my husband of 35 years, my heart. Thank you for all your contributions and your creative insights and especially your photography for the cover. I appreciate all the space you have given me during the process of writing. The absolute true love and awesome support you've given, has been more than words can express. You have always made me feel safe and you trust me, as much as I trust you. I dedicate this book to you. I love you.

APPENDIX 1

Expanding Visualization

Some people say they can't visualize, but then I ask them to describe their car or their home and they can do that easily. Well, that, my friend, is visualization.

Let's take a minute to do a visualization meditation. To start, close your eyes and take some deep breaths.

Now try breathing in for a count of four, hold for count of three, release breath to a count of four, then repeat. Let's try it together: breath in 1, 2, 3, 4 … hold for 1, 2, 3 … release for 1, 2, 3, 4. Again, breathe in 1, 2, 3, 4 … hold 1, 2, 3… and release 1, 2, 3, 4.

As you continue to breathe like this, I now want you to visualize a wrapped gift box with a big bow around it. It can be wrapped any way you want, maybe in something shiny, maybe just white or another solid color, maybe a patterned gift wrap—just try to focus on a picture of a wrapped gift box, any size or shape, with a big bow on it.

Breathe in, breathe out.

Every one of us has a gift or talent to share with the world, so I want you to visualize that gift that you can give, which is now inside that box. See the box still wrapped and the bow around it, but your gift or talent to the world is inside the box. Take a few seconds to really see it inside the box. Feel what it would feel like for you to give this wrapped gift box to someone.

Breathe in, breathe out.

Now visualize the bow being untied from this gift box, and the paper being taken off the box. Now you slowly see the top of the box being opened. As you open it, light starts to peak through, and as the top of the box is fully open, you see the light shine so bright all around it. The light shines into the sky; it shines all around you and everyone that you love and care about. It shines on all the new people you will meet this year. It shines on all the goals you create and achieve. It shines until there is no darkness at all.

Now slowly come back to your breathing. Take one more deep breath and then open your eyes. How did that feel for you?

INNER BEING IN BALANCE Workshops

The acronym BALANCE is made up of the seven principles I manifested to align myself with the universe and create the life of my dreams. Here is an easy breakdown of the 7 principles that I use in my workshops. www.healloveyourlife.com

1. Believing

Start with silence or meditating on your beliefs about yourself. Have a clear state of mind. Go deep inside your heart to truly feel the feelings of what you want to achieve. Rehearse your day with optimum mindset.

Close your eyes and ask yourself what is the primary objective to get what you want out of your day. What are your beliefs about this optimal situation? To show up for yourself, you need to put yourself in the best optimal feeling to achieve your day. Believing in yourself is the start to believing in everything. Remind yourself that you are doing your best. Ask yourself, "Who can help today?" and believe that the right person or situation will be presented to you. Once you believe, you will achieve. Acting and feeling "as if" will empower your belief.

2. Allowing

After meditation or even during meditation, allow feelings and emotions to enter your physical and emotional self. With the practice of allowing, you will become more intuitive to your needs and desires. Your energy of least resistance is when you start your day with an open mind and allow all the good that you are radiating to mirror the good in others. Allowing will help attract to you the goals you set for the day. Let go of any complaining or resistance. Open your arms wide in a *V* and say "I allow all good things to enter my life today."

3. Learning

Having an open mind and an enthusiastic thirst for knowledge is the best daily habit for creating the work and life you love. Our natural desire to create can be sparked through learning, reading, and writing. Reading something positive to start your day will put you in a state of mind of more positivity. Your frequency or vibe will only be enhanced through journaling or writing down your goals or aspirations for the day. Our intuitive or true self will emerge from this daily practice because you are on a path of learning to become your higher self.

4. Affirming

Each day after meditation, reading, and journaling, you will start practicing the art of affirmations. Affirmations are statements that we make, either positive or negative. Too often our thoughts are negative. Negative affirmations only create more of what we don't want. Positive affirmations will only open channels in our consciousness to create more of that.

Make positive statements about how you want your life to be. One important point: always make your statements in the present tense, such as "I am" or "I have" or "I enjoy." Saying "I will" or "I should" will only put your subconscious mind into the future tense. Saying "I want" or "I will" puts you out of reach and into future instead of the now. Try to eliminate the word *should* from your vocabulary and use the word *could*. It is a fun exercise when affirming.

5. Nurturing

Eating, exercising, and not condemning yourself is the path to nurturing and loving who you really are and who you choose to be. Start your day with a healthy breakfast or shake. Get your blood flowing by moving your body, whether it's yoga, stretching, running, walking dogs, dancing, or riding a bike. Let your exercise guide you, easily, with a state of mind of enjoyment instead of dread or sore muscles.

Start with ease in mind and build up every day to more of what your body can take. Don't give up or give in. Coach yourself by using your affirmations out loud or in your mind. Love who you are right now, in this present moment. Say *I love you* to yourself in the mirror.

Correct, but don't protect. Discover what your body needs by listening daily to nurture your physical, emotional, and soulful desires. Selfcare is more important now than ever in the automated and technological world we live in. Make it a morning habit to look at emails, scan social media, or answer the phone at least an hour after you wake up.

6. Celebrating

Each day before heading out into the "real world," think of one thing you have accomplished the day before and then celebrate it with thanks. Being grateful every day is a pure practice of celebration. The more grateful you are, the more great-full your life becomes, and the more reasons you will have to celebrate.

Giving is a form of celebrating. You give love by celebrating your life with others. Listening to music, dancing, and laughing are all forms of celebrating your life. Seeking adventure with a passion is also celebrating life. After affirming what you desire your life to be, manifesting is the step that follows. Once the manifestation of your desires has been met, celebrating the accomplishment will only bring more passion and adventure into your life. So, in essence, you are celebrating in every moment.

7. Expanding

We have all heard, "What you focus on expands." After you have made the first six habits into a daily ritual, your focus on them will expand to all areas of your life. Visualization is a way to help with expanding your thoughts and will help you focus on exactly what you want for the work and life you wish to create. Visualization is the process of using your imagination to achieve a desired result. Put most simply, you see what you want to happen in your mind first, before it actually does happen.

For example, if you want a new place to live, picture a house or an apartment that you desire, being as specific as possible. Then see it as if it were already true. Affirm that you deserve it. See your new home with you in it, going about your new daily routine. Practice your visualization every day, then turn the results over to the universe and ask for your highest good. Combined with your beliefs, allowing, learning, affirmations, nurturing, and celebrating, visualization will expand your focus.

Testimonial from an attendee of the 30 Day Challenge to Inner Being in BALANCE -

I participated in focusing on the BALANCE challenge/concept early in the year. I would be remiss not to say that it sat on my night table for 10 days after it was given to me. I spend a lot of energy worrying about the how instead of jumping in. And then I started and the magic happened. I believe I do healthy things and lead a healthy life yet at the same time burying my head in the sand or pretending I don't have some unhealthy habits. Using the BALANCE guidelines and tracker became a fun sort of game to me. Checking in each night before going to bed and realizing I do more than I think I do as well as encouraging me to try new methods. Most importantly, it encouraged me to have fun and celebrate. I think the most poignant part of the program, is that it slowed me down and honed my observation skills, aka encouraged mindfulness. I have a habitual stream of unkind thoughts about my performance, productivity and emotions. By sitting down every evening to compare my day with the 30 day tracker, I was able to congratulate myself and be kind seeing that "I am not so bad." and the majority of the days I touched on all aspects of an Inner Balance, giving me such peace and joy in my heart.

That calm peacefulness allowed me to shed the self-loathing, the perfection and unrealistic standards I put upon myself. I feel and know by doing this tracker it resets my thinking and helped me allow several miracles to happen a few months afterwards and during COVID-19.

BALANCE helped me to take some time at both the beginning and ending of each day to set intentions, ask for what I want, review events, see my emotions and call out my negative self-talk and note my positives all of which undoubtedly helped me attract incredible beauty.

I have been a fan and have participated in a lot of healing and self-development modalities. I liked Graves' philosophy, because it was done with a 30 day challenge. I see myself doing it once a year, using her tool simply to reinforce the practices I do daily.

This is something I highly recommend, if you would like to elevate to the next level.

Also, make it fun. Sometimes for "celebrate" I would note that I sang in the car or danced in front of the mirror laughing with myself. For all you perfectionists out there, it doesn't have to be complicated - that was my biggest take away.

Courtney Cotton

Artist - Denver Colorado

About the Author

*M*y name is Monica Graves. I was born in 1963. I graduated college with a BBA, and I have been an entrepreneur for past twenty-seven years. I am a mother of two charming boys and have been married to my college sweetheart, for 35 years. We are happily living with our 2 dogs and cat at our Retreat Gemstone Grand, in Grand Lake, CO.

I am a licensed Employing Broker for Your Castle Mountain Properties, Inc., where I work with my husband and my oldest son selling real estate in Vail, Winter Park, and Denver, Colorado. We also fix and flip homes for fun. Our website is www.purplemtn.com

I am also a licensed "Heal Your Life" workshop leader based on the philosophy of Louise Hay, where I teach others in workshops how to love their life (www.healloveyourlife.com).

I am in the top 2 percent of realtors nationwide and hold several designations. I have won the platinum award for earning $300,000–$500,000 in commission in 2016. 2017, 2018, and 2019. My success has been balancing my work with my life, attracting friends and clients into my business, and forming lifelong relationships with them. I hold weekly training sessions in mindset and accountability to help others achieve their goals. The attendance to these workshops and classes has exceeded over three thousand people in the last ten years.

My goal with writing this book, Inner Being In Balance, is to have many workshops and playshops, based on the 7 principles of Manifesting Success in Life, Business and Beyond! For dates and times, visit my website at www.innerbeinginbalance.com

PUBLICATIONS by Monica Graves

Weekly blog to thousands of Realtors, buyers, and sellers – www.purplemtn.com (2011-current)

Article in Health Magazine – "How I got healthy" 2007

Article in Science of Mind Magazine – "Raphael" 2006

Printed in the United States
By Bookmasters